Engage and Thrive

A Guide to Building a Strong Online Community
of Raving Fans

Veronica Goldspiel

Copyright © 2024 Veronica Goldspiel

All rights reserved.

All rights reserved. No part of this publication may be reproduced, distributed, or transmitted in any form or by any means, including photocopying, recording, or other electronic or mechanical methods, or by any information storage and retrieval system without prior written permission of the publisher, except in the case of very brief quotations embodied in critical reviews and certain other noncommercial uses permitted by copyright law.

This book is designed to provide accurate and authoritative information regarding the subject matter herein. It is sold with the understanding that the author and publisher are not engaged in rendering legal, accounting, or other professional services. If you require legal advice or other expert assistance, you should seek the services of a competent professional.

While the author has made every effort to provide accurate website addresses and other information at the time of publication, neither the publisher nor the author assumes any responsibility for errors or changes that occur after publication. Further, the publisher does not have any control over and does not assume any responsibility for author or third-party websites or their content.

Book Cover by Veronica Goldspiel

1st Edition 2024

Disclaimer

This publication is designed to provide accurate and authoritative information with regard to the subject matter covered. It is sold with the understanding that the publisher is not engaged in rendering legal, accounting, or other professional advice. If legal advice or other expert assistance is required, the services of a competent professional should be sought.

The author wishes to acknowledge the respective sources for use of graphs, charts, and other data in this book, and it is the author's intent to portray that data accurately rather than through representations.

This book may contain technical or other errors. Veronica Goldspiel and GCE Publishing do not guarantee its accuracy, completeness, or suitability. In no event shall Veronica Goldspiel and GCE Publishing be liable for any special, indirect, or consequential damages relating to this material for any use of this material or for any referenced website and courses, or the application of any idea or strategy in this book.

The information contained in this book is provided by Veronica Goldspiel and GCE Publishing, and it is offered for educational and informational purposes only. Veronica Goldspiel is a not a licensed financial planner. She suggests that you consult with a qualified legal or tax-planning professional with regard to your personal circumstances. Nothing in this book should be interpreted or construed as legal, regulatory, insurance, tax, or financial planning advice or as an offer to perform services related to any of these fields in any respect.

The content of this book contains general information and may not reflect current legal, tax, insurance, or regulatory developments and information, and it is not guaranteed to be correct, complete, or current. Veronica Goldspiel and GCE Publishing make no warranty, expressed or implied, as to the accuracy or reliability of this information or the information contained in any referenced website or course.

Readers of this book should not act or refrain from acting on the basis of any information included herein without seeking appropriate legal or other relevant advice related to the particular facts and circumstances at issue from an attorney or other advisor duly and properly licensed in the recipient's state of residence. Veronica Goldspiel and GCE Publishing expressly disclaim all liability with respect to actions taken or not taken by the reader based on any or all of the information or other contents within this book or provided by Veronica Goldspiel directly. Any information sent to Veronica Goldspiel or GCE Publishing via Internet, e-mail, or through any referenced website is not secure and is done so on a non-confidential basis.

Should the reader of this book seek a referral to any service provider, the person to whom such referral is made is solely responsible for assessing the knowledge, skill, or capabilities of such provider, and neither the author, presenter, nor Veronica Goldspiel, GCE Publishing are responsible for the quality, integrity, performance, or any other aspect of any services ultimately provided by such provider or any damages, consequential or incidental, arising from the use of such provider. Any opinions expressed in the book are mine alone and mine based on the information publicly available to me in my interpretation of that information.

DEDICATION

This book is dedicated to my husband, Alan, for always being an inspiration to me! I am so lucky to have you by my side! Love you!

Contents

FREE GIFT FOR MY READERS	VIII
Introduction: Engage and Thrive in the Digital Landscape	1
Chapter 1: The Power of Social Media for Small Business	5
Chapter 2: Understanding Your Audience	11
Chapter 3: Crafting Your Brand's Voice and Message	19
Chapter 4: Choosing The Right Platforms	27
Chapter 5: Content is King: Creating Engaging Posts That Convert	33
Chapter 6: Building an Engaged Community	39
Chapter 7: Social Media Growth Strategies	45
Chapter 8: Leveraging User-GeneratedContent and Social Proof	51
Chapter 9: Managing and Automating Your Social Media	57
Chapter 10: Analyzing and Measuring Success	63
Chapter 11: Handling Negative Feedback and Online Crises	71
Chapter 12: The Future of Social Media for Small Businesses	77
Conclusion: Engage, Thrive, and Lead the Way Forward	83
PLEASE DO ME A HUGE FAVOR	88
REMINDER	89
ABOUT THE AUTHOR	91
OTHER BOOKS BY AUTHOR	93

FREE GIFT FOR MY READERS

As a thank you for your support, I invite you to download some exciting FREE gifts that I've created to enhance your journey! Simply visit the link below to access exclusive resources designed just for you!

Your complimentary gifts include:

Engage and Thrive Cheat Sheet – This is your quick-reference guide to social media success! This valuable resource keeps essential strategies top of mind—from defining goals and knowing your audience to creating engaging content and managing feedback. Use it to stay focused on building a loyal, active community that drives your brand forward!

Handling Negative Feedback Cheat Sheet – This your essential resource for staying poised and professional in the face of criticism! This quick guide serves as a valuable reminder of key steps to take when managing feedback—from acknowledging concerns to turning insights into improvement. Keep it handy to protect your brand's reputation while building stronger relationships through thoughtful responses!

Social Proof Cheat Sheet for Small Businesses – This is your must-have guide to boosting credibility and trust with potential customers! This valuable resource covers key ways to gather and showcase authentic feedback, testimonials, and influencer endorsements that make your brand stand out. Keep it on hand to easily remind yourself of proven strategies that build customer confidence and drive sales!

30-Day Social Media Content Calendar Cheat Sheet – This is your ultimate roadmap to creating meaningful, high-engagement content every day! This valuable resource will keep you inspired with fresh ideas that foster connection, showcase your brand, and build an active, thriving community. It's the perfect guide to remind you of key strategies and take your social presence to the next level!

GET YOUR FREE GIFTS NOW BY GOING TO: https://goldspielcreativeenterprises.com/free-gifts-engage-and-thrive/

CONNECT WITH ME ON FACEBOOK!

Join my *Small Business Wealth Marketing* private Facebook community here: https://www.facebook.com/groups/smallbusinesswealthmarketing

I also invite you to engage with me on my Official Veronica Goldspiel Author Facebook Page here: https://www.facebook.com/veronicagoldspielauthor/

Introduction: Engage and Thrive in the Digital Landscape

"Social media is one area of business where you don't need to outspend your competitors in order to beat them."

-Hal Stokes

In the dynamic world of social media, where trends shift at lightning speed and engagement is the currency of success, the journey of connecting with your audience can feel overwhelming. As someone who has navigated this terrain for over a decade—working as a social media manager for a digital agency and serving multiple clients as a freelance social media strategist—I've witnessed firsthand the transformative power of effective social media engagement. The knowledge and experience I've gained along this journey inspired me to write *Engage and Thrive: A Guide to Building a Strong Online Community of Raving Fans*, the second installment in my Small Business Wealth Marketing Series.

This book follows the success of my first book, *From Likes to Profits*, which achieved Amazon's #1 Best Seller status. The overwhelming response showed me that many small businesses and freelancers are searching for practical strategies to navigate the social media landscape and turn followers into loyal customers. It became clear that there is a deep need for actionable insights that not only elevate online presence but also foster meaningful connections with audiences. This book is designed to address that need and provide you with the tools you require to thrive.

Why Social Media Matters for Small Businesses

In today's digital age, social media is not just a marketing tool; it's a vital lifeline for small businesses and freelancers. With over 4 billion people actively using social media platforms globally, these channels offer unprecedented access to a vast audience. For small businesses and freelancers, social media is an opportunity to tell your story, share your values, and connect with customers on a personal level. The landscape is rich with possibilities, yet it can be daunting without a clear strategy.

Here are some compelling reasons why mastering social media is essential for your success:

1. **Build Brand Awareness:** Social media platforms allow you to introduce your brand to potential customers who may not otherwise discover you. Consistent and engaging content helps establish your brand's presence and fosters recognition in a crowded marketplace.

2. **Engage with Your Audience:** Unlike traditional advertising methods, social media provides a unique platform for two-way communication. Engaging with your audience fosters loyalty and trust, as customers appreciate brands that listen and respond to their needs.

3. **Showcase Your Expertise:** By sharing valuable insights, tips, and stories related to your industry, you position yourself as an expert in your field. This builds credibility and encourages potential clients to see you as a valuable resource.

4. **Drive Traffic and Conversions:** Well-crafted social media strategies can lead followers directly to your website or landing pages. By providing clear calls to action and enticing offers, you can convert followers into customers.

5. **Cultivate Community:** Social media is about creating a community around your brand. When your audience feels connected to you and each other, they become more likely to advocate for your business, amplifying your reach through word-of-mouth marketing.

Unlocking the Potential of Your Business

In *Engage and Thrive*, I will share proven strategies and tactics that can significantly improve your social media presence and, in turn, your business performance. This book will guide you in understanding how to effectively engage your audience, leverage user-generated content, manage your social media efficiently, analyze your performance, and even handle negative feedback with grace.

Throughout my career, I have helped many small businesses and freelancers harness the power of social media to drive growth. The techniques and insights presented in this book are not just theoretical—they are practical, actionable steps that I have implemented successfully for my clients. Here are just a few ways these strategies can enhance your business:

- **Increase Engagement:** By creating content that resonates with your audience, you'll foster deeper connections, resulting in higher engagement rates.

- **Streamline Management:** Efficiently managing your social media presence will free up your time, allowing you to focus on what truly matters—growing your business and serving your clients.

- **Enhance Your Brand's Image:** A strong social media presence will elevate your brand's image, making it more appealing to potential customers and partners.

- **Build a Loyal Community:** Cultivating an engaged community means you'll have a group of loyal supporters ready to advocate for your business.

The Structure of This Book

Engage and Thrive is designed to be a comprehensive guide, breaking down complex strategies into digestible sections that you can easily implement. Each chapter will focus on a key aspect of social media management, providing actionable insights, real-world examples, and inspirational anecdotes to motivate you on your journey.

From understanding the importance of user-generated content to analyzing your performance metrics, this book will equip you with the knowledge and confidence you need to make informed decisions about your social media strategy. Each chapter concludes with actionable steps, allowing you to apply what you've learned immediately.

Inspiration for Your Journey

As you embark on this journey to enhance your social media presence, remember that success doesn't happen overnight. It's a continuous process of learning, adapting, and growing. Celebrate the small victories along the way, and don't shy away from challenges—they are the stepping stones to your success.

Be authentic, be consistent, and be engaged. Your voice matters, and your passion can shine through every post, every comment, and every interaction you have online. By leveraging the insights in this book, you'll not only enhance your social media skills but also create a thriving online community that champions your brand.

Let's Get Started

I invite you to take a deep breath and step into the possibilities that await you. The world of social media is filled with opportunities for connection, growth, and impact. As you turn the pages of *Engage and Thrive*, remember that you are not alone on this journey. Many others are navigating this landscape with the same hopes and dreams, and together, we can build vibrant online communities that uplift and inspire.

Thank you for joining me in this endeavor. Let's embark on this journey together, and I look forward to seeing your brand flourish as you engage, thrive, and lead the way forward in the digital landscape.

Chapter 1: The Power of Social Media for Small Business

"Social media is about sociology and psychology more than technology."

-Brian Solis

In today's world, social media is not just a tool—it's a *superpower* for small businesses and freelancers. Whether you're a one-person operation working out of your home office or a small business hustling to grow, social media has become a critical element in your success. The days of relying on costly advertising or hoping for word-of-mouth growth are over. With social media, you have a platform that allows you to reach a massive audience, build relationships, and convert followers into loyal customers—all without breaking the bank.

Why Social Media is Non-Negotiable

Let's face it: if you're not active on social media, you're leaving money and opportunities on the table. We're living in a digital age where people turn to social platforms like Instagram, Facebook, and LinkedIn to discover new brands, engage with businesses, and make purchasing decisions. And we're not just talking about younger generations here. Everyone, from teenagers to grandparents, is scrolling through social media, looking for solutions to their problems.

For small businesses, this is a *goldmine*. You don't need a million-dollar marketing budget. You just need a solid strategy, a clear message, and a willingness to engage. Unlike traditional advertising methods, social media allows you to interact with your audience in real time, giving you a direct line of communication that can significantly boost your business.

Here's the beauty of it: social media is democratic. Whether you're a huge corporation or a small business, the playing field is surprisingly level. It's no longer about who has the biggest billboard or the most expensive ad campaign. It's about who can connect with their audience in the most authentic and engaging way.

Leveling the Playing Field: Big Business Versus Small Business

Think back to the pre-social media days. If you were a small business owner, you were competing with giant corporations that had way more money, resources, and reach. Competing with them was like trying to knock down Goliath with a slingshot. But social media has changed the game.

Today, small businesses have the unique opportunity to shine brighter than ever before. You don't need a massive budget; you just need to be *authentic*. That's the magic of social media. Customers crave connection, and small businesses have the advantage of being able to offer a more personal touch than larger brands.

Take, for example, the story of a local bakery that started posting photos of its beautifully crafted cupcakes on Instagram. They didn't have a huge marketing team or a big advertising budget, but they understood one thing: *engagement is key*. Through regular posts, interacting with followers, and sharing behind-the-scenes stories, this bakery developed a loyal following that ultimately led to significant business growth. And the best part? They did it all on a shoestring budget.

When you're a small business or freelancer, you have the ability to pivot quickly, respond personally to customer comments, and create a brand story that resonates on a deeper level. Large corporations may have bigger budgets, but you have something far more valuable: the ability to build genuine connections.

The Benefits of Social Media for Small Businesses

Now that we've established why social media is such a game-changer, let's dig into the specific benefits it offers small businesses and freelancers. These advantages can set the foundation for your long-term growth and success.

Brand Visibility: Shine Bright in a Crowded Market

Social media is one of the most powerful tools for getting your brand in front of the right people. Every time you post, comment, or share, you're increasing the visibility of your business. Think of it as casting a wide net in a sea of potential customers. But instead of relying on traditional marketing channels (which can be expensive and hard to measure), social media allows you to directly reach your target audience in real time.

When you're active on social media, people start to recognize your brand. It may begin as a casual glance at a post, but over time, as your content appears regularly in their feed, your brand becomes familiar. And in marketing, familiarity breeds trust. Once people trust your brand, they're far more likely to make a purchase.

It doesn't stop at just being seen. Your content, whether it's a video, a blog post, or a simple image, can be shared, and shared again. One great post can get in front of hundreds or even thousands of new people, all because someone decided to hit the "share" button.

Direct Communication: Get to Know Your Customers

The old marketing adage used to be "spray and pray." You'd send out a message through a billboard, a TV ad, or a flyer and hope that the right people saw it. Social media flipped that script entirely.

Now, small businesses can have a direct line of communication with their audience. And this communication isn't just a one-way street. It's interactive. You can have conversations with your customers. You can ask for feedback, answer questions, and offer personalized recommendations. This real-time communication gives you insights into your audience's needs, preferences, and behaviors in a way that traditional marketing could never achieve.

And here's the kicker: customers *love* it when brands engage with them. It makes them feel heard, valued, and part of something bigger than just a transaction. By responding to comments, liking posts, and engaging with user-generated content, you can build a sense of community around your brand. And that's where loyalty starts.

When customers feel like they're a part of your brand's journey, they're far more likely to stick around—and even become ambassadors for your business.

Customer Loyalty: Turning Followers into Superfans

It's one thing to get someone to follow you on social media; it's another to turn them into a loyal, repeat customer. The magic of social media is that it offers small businesses the opportunity to build long-term relationships with their audience, which is the foundation of customer loyalty.

How do you do this? By showing up consistently, providing value, and engaging with your audience. Remember, social media isn't just about broadcasting your products or services—it's about building a connection. People are drawn to brands that are authentic, transparent, and relatable. When you regularly post content that resonates with your audience, they begin to feel a sense of loyalty to your brand.

And here's the best part: loyal customers are your best marketers. They'll tell their friends, share your posts, and sing your praises to anyone who will listen. One loyal customer can bring in a whole new wave of business without you ever having to spend a dime on advertising. That's the power of building a community around your brand.

Building Your Social Media Strategy

Now that we've covered the benefits of social media for small businesses, it's time to start thinking about your strategy. Success doesn't happen by accident. It takes planning, consistency, and a deep understanding of your audience.

Here are a few quick tips to get you started on the right path:

- **Start with a Clear Goal**: What do you want to achieve with social media? Are you looking to increase brand awareness, drive sales, or build a community? Having a clear goal will help guide your content and engagement strategy.

- **Be Consistent**: Success on social media doesn't happen overnight. It requires consistency. Post regularly, engage with your audience, and don't be afraid to experiment with different types of content.

- **Provide Value**: Don't make every post a sales pitch. Offer value to your audience through educational content, entertainment, or behind-the-scenes insights. The more value you provide, the more likely your audience is to engage with you.

- **Engage with Your Followers**: Social media is a two-way street. Don't just post and ghost. Respond to comments, ask questions, and be part of the conversation.

- **Track Your Progress**: Use analytics to monitor your performance. What types of posts are getting the most engagement? What time of day do you get the most interactions? Use this data to refine your strategy over time.

Embrace the Power of Social Media

In a world where consumers are constantly bombarded with advertising messages, social media offers small businesses a way to stand out and build genuine connections with their audience. It's more than just a marketing tool; it's a platform for storytelling, engagement, and community-building.

The power of social media lies in its ability to give small businesses a voice—and an audience willing to listen. If you're ready to take your business to the next level, social media is the key to unlocking that growth. With the right strategy, you can turn followers into fans, and fans into lifelong customers. Your journey to building a thriving online community starts now!

Stay tuned for the next chapter, where we'll dive into understanding your audience and crafting the perfect message to connect with them on a deeper level.

Chapter 2: Understanding Your Audience

> *"People want to do business with you because you help them get what they want. They don't do business with you to help you get what you want."*
>
> -Don Crowther

Building a strong online presence and creating a thriving community of raving fans starts with one crucial element: *understanding your audience*. You can have the most polished brand, the flashiest content, and even an irresistible product or service, but if you aren't connecting with the right people, your social media efforts are going to fall flat.

Think of it like this: Imagine throwing a party and sending out a ton of invitations to people who don't share your interests. Sure, you might get a few people to show up, but chances are, they won't stick around for long because they don't connect with what you're offering. The same holds true for social media. You need to know who you're talking to, what they care about, and how to keep them engaged.

Identifying Your Target Audience Through Market Research

To craft a social media strategy that truly resonates, you first need to identify your *target audience*—those people who are most likely to benefit from your product or service. These are the people who will feel an emotional connection to your brand, follow you eagerly, and eventually become your biggest fans and customers.

So, how do you go about identifying this target audience? The answer lies in good old-fashioned market research. But don't worry—it's easier (and a lot more fun) than it sounds.

Step 1: Start With Who You Already Know

If you're a small business or freelancer, you probably already have some customers or clients. These people are your goldmine of information. Take some time to look at your current customer base and ask yourself a few key questions:

- What do they have in common?
- What age group do they belong to?
- Where are they from?
- What problems are they looking to solve?

You might notice patterns emerging. For example, if you're a graphic designer who primarily works with local businesses, you may find that most of your clients are small business owners in their 30s and 40s who need branding help. That's a great start in defining your audience!

Step 2: Dig Deeper with Surveys and Polls

Social media makes it easy to interact with your audience in real time, and one of the best ways to gather valuable information is through surveys and polls. You can use platforms like Instagram Stories, Twitter, or Facebook to ask your followers questions directly.

Some questions you could ask include:

- What type of content would you like to see more of?
- What are your biggest challenges in [insert your industry]?
- How do you prefer to interact with brands on social media?

By actively listening to your audience, you can gather insights that will help shape your future content and offerings.

Step 3: **Competitive Research**

Another great way to identify your target audience is by looking at what your competitors are doing. Who is engaging with their posts? What kind of content resonates with their followers? Tools like BuzzSumo and Sprout Social can help you analyze your competitors' performance and give you a better understanding of the types of people you should be targeting.

The Power of Customer Personas: How to Create Them and Why They Matter

Once you've gathered all this valuable information, it's time to take it a step further by creating *customer personas*. Think of these as fictional profiles that represent your ideal customers. They're like avatars for the types of people you want to attract, and they'll help guide all of your social media and marketing efforts.

Why Customer Personas Matter

Customer personas are essential because they help you personalize your content and messaging. When you know exactly who you're talking to, it's easier to craft content that speaks directly to their needs, interests, and pain points. Instead of casting a wide net and hoping to catch a few fish, you're targeting the exact people who are most likely to engage with your brand.

How to Create Customer Personas

Creating a customer persona is all about combining the data you've collected with a little imagination. Here's how to do it:

1. **Give Your Persona a Name and Job Title** To make your persona feel real, start by giving them a name. Let's say you run a yoga studio; you might create a persona named *Megan*, who's a busy professional in her mid-30s. Megan's job title might be something like "Marketing Manager," which gives you insight into her lifestyle and work habits.

2. **Demographic Information** Next, add some demographic details like:

- Age: 35

- Gender: Female

- Location: Urban area

- Income: $75,000/year

- Education: Bachelor's degree

3. **Pain Points** What are Megan's biggest challenges or frustrations? For example, Megan might struggle with stress and finding time for self-care, which makes her an ideal candidate for yoga classes.

4. **Goals and Motivations** What does Megan want to achieve? Maybe she's looking for a way to balance her hectic work life with a healthier lifestyle. This goal will inform the type of content you create, like posts about quick yoga routines that fit into a busy schedule.

5. **Preferred Social Media Platforms** Where does Megan spend her time online? Maybe she's an avid Instagram user who follows fitness influencers, which tells you where you should focus your efforts to reach her.

Here's what Megan's persona might look like:

Megan Carter, Marketing Manager

- Age: 35

- Location: New York City

- Goals: To reduce stress and improve overall well-being

- Challenges: Busy work schedule, lack of time for self-care

- Preferred Platforms: Instagram, YouTube

- Interests: Fitness, wellness, mindfulness

Now, every time you create content for your social media channels, you can ask yourself, "What would resonate with Megan?" Having this persona in mind ensures that your messaging is targeted and effective.

Using Social Media Analytics to Refine Audience Understanding

Creating customer personas is just the beginning. As your social media presence grows, it's essential to continuously refine your understanding of your audience, and social media analytics are your best friend in this process.

Platforms like Facebook, Instagram, and Twitter provide in-depth analytics that give you insight into who's interacting with your content. By analyzing metrics such as age, gender, location, and engagement patterns, you can fine-tune your personas and content strategies.

Using Data to Refine Your Strategy

Let's say you've been posting regularly on Instagram and notice that your posts about behind-the-scenes content are getting the most engagement. That's a clue that your audience wants more authenticity and transparency from your brand. Or perhaps you discover that your posts perform better on weekday evenings—this tells you when your audience is most active and when you should be posting.

By continuously monitoring your social media analytics, you can adjust your content to better meet the needs and preferences of your audience. For a more in-depth guide on how to use social media analytics to grow your business, check out my book *From Likes to Profits*. In it, I break down the most critical metrics to track and show you how to interpret the data to drive better results.

Real-World Example: Lush Cosmetics

Lush Cosmetics is an excellent example of a brand that knows how to engage with its audience on social media. They've built a loyal following by creating personas that reflect their customers' values and interests. Lush's audience is made up of eco-conscious individuals who care about ethical sourcing, sustainability, and cruelty-free products. By understanding their audience deeply, Lush is able to craft content that resonates.

Their social media posts often focus on behind-the-scenes looks at how their products are made, customer testimonials, and initiatives related to sustainability. They don't just sell soap; they sell a lifestyle that aligns with their audience's values.

Lush also makes great use of social media analytics to refine their strategy. They noticed that posts about environmental impact got significantly higher engagement, so they doubled down on that type of content. They've successfully built a community of raving fans by listening to their audience and providing the type of content they care about.

Tips and Tricks

Now that you understand the importance of knowing your audience, here are a few tips, tricks, and action steps to help you get started:

Tip: Use Polls and Surveys Don't guess what your audience wants—ask them! Use Instagram Stories, Facebook polls, or Twitter to gather real-time feedback from your followers.

Tip: Follow Competitors Keep an eye on what your competitors are doing. It can give you valuable insights into what works (and what doesn't) for a similar audience.

Trick: Pay Attention to Comments Your comment section is a treasure trove of insights. Pay attention to what people are saying and asking for. This can give you a clear idea of what content to create next.

Action Steps

Action Step 1: Create a Customer Persona Take the time to develop 2-3 customer personas that represent your ideal audience. Use them as a guide for crafting your social media content.

Action Step 2: Analyze Your Analytics Dive into your social media analytics this week. Look for trends in who is engaging with your content, when they're most active, and what types of posts get the most traction. Adjust your strategy accordingly.

Conclusion: Knowing Your Audience is Key to Success

Understanding your audience isn't just important—it's *essential* to the success of your social media strategy. By identifying your target audience, creating customer personas, and using data to refine your strategy, you'll be able to create content that resonates, engages, and ultimately converts followers into loyal fans.

In the next chapter, we'll dive into crafting the perfect message for your audience—because once you know who you're talking to, it's all about saying the right things to keep them engaged. Stay tuned!

Chapter 3: Crafting Your Brand's Voice and Message

"Everything you post on social media impacts your brand. How do you want to be known?"

-Lisa Horn

Crafting your brand's voice and message is like finding your social media "superpower." Your voice is how your audience hears and perceives you online, and your message is the story you're telling. Nail both of these, and you'll have the key to standing out in a crowded marketplace.

For small businesses and freelancers, creating a unique voice is more than just choosing a few words that sound cool. It's about defining who you are, what you stand for, and how you'll communicate consistently across platforms. When done right, your voice becomes a beacon that draws in your target audience, makes them feel connected to you, and transforms casual followers into raving fans.

Defining Your Brand's Unique Personality Online

Your brand's voice is your personality on social media. Think of your brand as a person: how would they talk, act, and engage with others? Are they fun and quirky, or professional and polished? Understanding the unique personality of your brand helps create a voice that feels authentic and relatable.

Step 1: Know Who You Are

Before you can figure out how to talk to your audience, you need to understand who you are as a brand. Your brand's identity should reflect your values, mission, and the experience you want your customers to have.

Ask yourself these questions:

- What are your core values?
- What emotions do you want to evoke in your audience?
- How do you want people to describe your brand?

For example, if you're a freelance graphic designer who focuses on modern, edgy design, your voice might be bold, creative, and a bit playful. On the other hand, if you're a small accounting firm, your voice may lean more toward professionalism, trustworthiness, and clarity.

Real-World Example: Wendy's

Wendy's, the fast-food chain, is known for having a sassy, humorous social media voice that's unlike any other in its industry. They've found success by being playful and unafraid to roast their competitors—something that reflects their bold and confident personality. This tone sets them apart, and their fans love it because it feels authentic to the brand. Wendy's doesn't try to sound like anyone else. They've honed a voice that is uniquely theirs.

Step 2: Understand Your Audience

Your voice isn't just about you; it's about how your audience hears you. Once you've identified your target audience (as discussed in the previous chapter), you'll want to match your voice to their preferences.

For instance, if your audience consists mostly of young, creative entrepreneurs, your voice might need to be casual, fun, and full of inspirational language. If you're catering to corporate professionals, a more formal tone might resonate better.

The key here is to find a balance: your voice should be authentic to your brand while also appealing to the people you're trying to reach.

Real-World Example: Mailchimp

Mailchimp, a marketing automation platform, has built its brand on being approachable and friendly. Their voice reflects this—whether they're sending emails or creating social media posts, they maintain a tone that's conversational, clear, and a little quirky. Their audience, made up of small business owners and freelancers, appreciates the simplicity and ease of use Mailchimp brings to an often-complicated process. This connection between voice and audience has helped Mailchimp build a loyal community.

Step 3: Find Your Tone

Your tone is the mood or feeling behind your words. While your brand's voice should remain consistent, your tone might shift depending on the context. For example, you might have a more serious tone when addressing customer service issues and a more lighthearted tone when celebrating an achievement.

A good rule of thumb is to be flexible with your tone but consistent with your voice.

Building Consistency Across Platforms

Consistency is key when it comes to crafting a strong brand voice. Your audience should be able to recognize your voice no matter where they interact with you—whether it's Instagram, LinkedIn, Twitter, or even your website. When your voice is consistent, it builds trust and makes your brand feel reliable.

Step 1: Create a Brand Voice Guide

One of the best ways to maintain consistency is to create a brand voice guide. This is essentially a cheat sheet that outlines your brand's voice and provides guidelines for how to communicate across all platforms. It should include:

- A description of your brand's personality

- Examples of the type of language you use (and don't use)

- Specific words or phrases that are part of your brand's identity

- Guidelines on tone and how it might change in different situations

Having this guide ensures that anyone managing your social media accounts or writing content for your business stays on-brand.

Step 2: Adapt Your Voice for Different Platforms

While consistency is important, it's also essential to understand the unique culture of each platform. The way you communicate on Twitter might differ slightly from how you engage on LinkedIn. For example, Twitter is fast-paced and more conversational, so a witty, concise tone might work well there. Meanwhile, LinkedIn is more professional, so your posts might be a bit more polished and focused on thought leadership.

The key is to adapt your content for each platform while keeping the same core voice. This flexibility allows you to connect with your audience in a way that feels natural for each social media space.

Real-World Example: Nike

Nike is a master of consistency across platforms. Whether you're on Instagram, Twitter, or YouTube, Nike's voice is always motivational, inspiring, and empowering. They've built their brand around the idea of pushing limits and celebrating athletes of all levels. Whether they're sharing a heartfelt video on YouTube or a punchy tweet, you can immediately recognize Nike's voice.

Tips for Writing Engaging and Authentic Posts That Connect with Your Audience

Now that you've nailed down your brand's voice and ensured it's consistent across platforms, it's time to start creating content that engages your audience. Here are some tips to help you write posts that connect:

1. **Be Authentic**

People can tell when you're faking it. In today's social media landscape, authenticity is one of the most important factors in building trust. Speak in a way that reflects your true brand identity, even if it means not being perfect all the time. Show behind-the-scenes moments, share your challenges, and be real with your audience.

2. Tell Stories

Humans are hardwired to connect through stories. Instead of just promoting your products or services, tell stories that illustrate the impact your brand has. Maybe it's a customer success story or a personal anecdote about your business journey. Stories are memorable, and they create an emotional connection with your audience.

Real-World Example: Patagonia

Outdoor brand Patagonia frequently shares stories of environmental activism and their commitment to sustainability. They don't just talk about the products they sell; they tell stories about the causes they believe in, which deeply resonates with their audience. This storytelling approach has helped them build a passionate community of loyal fans.

3. Speak Directly to Your Audience

When you write posts, imagine you're having a one-on-one conversation with your ideal customer. Use "you" language to make your audience feel like you're speaking directly to them. This creates a sense of connection and makes your posts feel more personal.

4. Use Emotion to Connect

Emotion is a powerful tool in creating engagement. Whether you're making your audience laugh, inspiring them, or even tugging at their heartstrings, emotions are what drive action. Don't be afraid to infuse emotion into your posts to create a deeper connection with your followers.

5. Keep It Simple and Clear

Social media is a fast-moving space. Your audience doesn't have time to read long, complicated posts. Keep your messaging simple, clear, and to the point. Use short sentences, bullet points, and visuals to get your message across quickly and effectively.

- Tips, Tricks, and Action Steps

- Now that you've learned the importance of your brand's voice and how to use it effectively, here are some actionable steps you can take today:

Tips

1. **Create a Voice Cheat Sheet:** Start by writing down five words that describe your brand's personality. Use these words as a guide when crafting social media posts.

2. **Batch Your Content:** Write a week's worth of posts in one sitting. This ensures that your voice stays consistent and helps you get into a creative flow.

3. **Engage in Conversations:** Social media isn't a one-way street. Respond to comments and messages in your brand's voice to build a stronger connection with your audience.

Tricks

1. **Repurpose Content:** Use the same core message across platforms, but tweak the tone and style to fit each one. For example, you might create an inspirational Instagram post and repurpose the message into a more detailed LinkedIn article.

2. **Use Emojis (Sparingly):** Depending on your brand's personality, emojis can be a fun way to add personality to your posts. Just make sure they're used strategically and don't overwhelm the message.

Action Steps

1. **Define Your Brand's Voice:** Take 30 minutes today to write a short description of your brand's voice. Ask yourself: What does your brand sound like? What tone do you want to convey? What emotions do you want to evoke?

2. **Create 2-3 Social Media Posts:** Using your brand's voice, create 2-3 posts for your preferred social media platform. Focus on telling a story or sharing a behind-the-scenes moment.

3. **Analyze Your Competitors' Voice:** Spend some time observing how your competitors communicate on social media. What works well for them? What doesn't? Use these insights to refine your own voice.

Let Your Voice Be Heard

Your brand's voice is your identity online. It's how people connect with you, remember you, and ultimately, become loyal customers. By defining your unique personality, maintaining consistency across platforms, and crafting engaging posts, you'll build an online presence that resonates with your audience. Now it's time to get started—let your voice be heard!

A Quick Note About the Difference Between Voice and Tone

It's easy to mix up "voice" and "tone," but here's a simple way to keep them straight. Your "voice" is the essence of who you are as a brand—it's your identity, values, and purpose. This doesn't change much. You might tweak it here and there, but overall, your voice stays consistent because it represents your core message and mission.

"Tone," on the other hand, is how you adjust that voice depending on the situation or audience. Think of it like this: you wouldn't speak to your boss the same way you'd chat with your best friend or family. The tone shifts depending on the context, but your voice—what you stand for and the values behind it—remains the same no matter who you're speaking to.

Chapter 4: Choosing The Right Platforms

"Social marketing eliminates the middlemen, providing brands the unique opportunity to have a direct relationship with their customers."

-Bryan Weiner

"In today's digital age, social media is no longer a "nice-to-have" but a "must-have" for small businesses and freelancers. However, one common mistake is thinking you need to be on every platform. The truth is, you don't have to be everywhere—you just need to be where your audience is. Choosing the right social media platforms for your business can make all the difference between spinning your wheels and gaining traction. In this chapter, we'll dive into the major platforms, how to pick the right ones for your brand, and ways to develop platform-specific strategies for maximum impact.

Overview of Major Social Media Platforms

Before you can decide which platforms are best for your business, it's important to understand the strengths and weaknesses of each one. Here's a quick overview of some of the major players in the social media game:

Facebook: Facebook is still one of the most popular platforms with over 2.9 billion users worldwide. It's great for businesses that want to build a community through groups, share longer-form content, and engage with a wide range of demographics. The platform is especially useful for B2C (business-to-consumer) businesses, as it allows for detailed audience targeting through paid ads. Think of it as a versatile platform for driving brand awareness and building a loyal following. I usually recommend that every brand/business have a Facebook page regardless of their product or service.

Instagram: If your business thrives on visuals, Instagram is a must. With its focus on photos, videos, and stories, it's the go-to platform for showcasing your brand's aesthetic. Instagram also skews younger, with the majority of its users between the ages of 18 and 34, making it perfect for brands targeting Millennials and Gen Z. Instagram's shopping features are ideal for eCommerce businesses looking to turn followers into buyers.

X (formerly known as Twitter): X is a fast-paced platform ideal for sharing news, quick updates, and engaging in real-time conversations. With its character limit, X forces you to get straight to the point, making it a great platform for businesses that want to showcase thought leadership, provide customer service, or participate in trending conversations. However, due to its rapid-fire nature, X requires frequent updates and engagement to stay relevant.

LinkedIn: LinkedIn is the professional's social network. It's ideal for B2B (business-to-business) businesses, freelancers, and professionals looking to build their network, share industry insights, or position themselves as experts in their field. If your business relies heavily on client relationships or professional services, LinkedIn is a goldmine.

TikTok: For brands targeting a younger audience and willing to get creative with short-form video, TikTok offers massive potential for organic reach. TikTok's algorithm is known for surfacing content to users who don't even follow you, which can lead to viral moments. It's especially useful for brands in fashion, entertainment, beauty, and food. However, this platform has been having security and government issues as of late so I would advise you to look into what's happening in your country. I usually don't recommend TikTok to any of my clients because they generally don't see much ROI (return on investment) when using it. I, personally, have never used this platform. However, if you feel it's a good fit for you and your brand, go for it.

Pinterest: If your business revolves around DIY, crafts, home decor, or recipes, Pinterest is a great platform to drive traffic to your website. Pinterest users are planners, and many use the platform to search for inspiration, so if your content aligns with that behavior, you'll see great results.

How to Choose the Best Platforms for Your Business

Now that you have a sense of what each platform offers, it's time to figure out which ones make the most sense for your business. Here are a few steps to guide your decision-making process:

Know Your Audience: Start by identifying where your audience hangs out. Refer back to your customer personas (as we discussed in Chapter 2) and figure out which platforms align with your target demographic. If you're targeting professionals or B2B clients, LinkedIn should be your focus. If you're selling products to Gen Z, TikTok or Instagram might be a better fit.

Understand Your Content Strengths: What kind of content does your brand excel at creating? If you're great at creating visual content, Instagram and Pinterest will serve you well. If you prefer writing thought-provoking articles or sharing professional insights, LinkedIn or Twitter may be more effective.

Assess Your Resources: It's important to be realistic about how much time and energy you can dedicate to each platform. If you're a small business or solo freelancer, managing five different platforms might be overwhelming. Instead, focus on two or three platforms where you can be most consistent and engaged.

Align with Your Goals: Think about what you want to achieve with your social media presence. Are you looking to drive traffic to your website? Build brand awareness? Generate leads? Some platforms, like Facebook and Instagram, offer robust advertising tools to help you drive conversions, while others, like Twitter, might be better for raising awareness and engaging in conversations.

Creating Platform-Specific Strategies for Maximum Impact

Once you've selected the platforms that make the most sense for your business, it's time to develop strategies tailored to each one. Here's how you can approach it:

Facebook Strategy: On Facebook, consider creating a business page and a community group. Pages are great for broadcasting updates and promoting products, while groups foster a sense of community and can be used for customer engagement. Also, leverage

Facebook's robust advertising tools to target specific demographics and interests with paid promotions.

Instagram Strategy: On Instagram, your focus should be on high-quality visuals and storytelling. Use Instagram Stories for behind-the-scenes content, polls, and Q&A sessions. Posts should reflect your brand's personality, and you can use Instagram Shopping to make your products easily accessible to customers. Consistency is key, so develop a content calendar to stay on top of regular posting.

Twitter Strategy: With Twitter, aim to be part of the conversation. Follow relevant hashtags, engage with influencers in your industry, and tweet frequently to stay visible. Share your insights on trending topics, retweet relevant content, and use Twitter's poll feature to engage your audience in real time.

LinkedIn Strategy: LinkedIn requires a more professional tone. Share industry insights, thought leadership articles, and professional achievements. Building relationships with other professionals is key, so don't be afraid to engage in discussions, comment on posts, and showcase your expertise in relevant LinkedIn groups.

Pinterest Strategy: On Pinterest, focus on creating visually appealing pins that link back to your website. Use keyword-rich descriptions and titles to make your pins discoverable. Pinterest works well with long-term content strategies, so focus on evergreen content that will continue to drive traffic to your site over time.

Real-World Example: Choosing the Right Platform

Let's look at a real-world example. A local bakery might choose to focus on Instagram and Pinterest because their business is highly visual. They can post photos of their beautifully decorated cakes, recipes, and behind-the-scenes videos of how their products are made. Pinterest can be used to link back to their website, where customers can place orders.

On the other hand, a freelance graphic designer targeting small businesses might focus more on LinkedIn and Instagram. LinkedIn allows them to showcase their portfolio in a professional context and network with potential clients, while Instagram gives them a platform to display their design work in a more creative, visual manner.

Tips and Tricks for Choosing Platforms

Start Small: Don't try to conquer every platform at once. Pick two or three to focus on, and expand as you grow.

Test and Adjust: Experiment with different platforms and see where you get the most engagement. Be flexible and ready to pivot based on what works.

Use Scheduling Tools: Tools like Hootsuite or Buffer can help you manage multiple platforms without feeling overwhelmed. These tools allow you to schedule posts in advance, saving you time and energy.

Action Steps to Get Started

1. **Identify Your Top Two Platforms:** Based on your audience, content strengths, and business goals, choose the two platforms that make the most sense for your brand.

2. **Develop Platform-Specific Goals:** For each platform, decide what you want to achieve. Do you want to increase followers, drive traffic to your website, or boost sales? Having clear goals will help you measure success.

3. **Create a Content Calendar:** Plan out your posts in advance for each platform. This will help you stay consistent and ensure that your messaging is aligned with your brand's voice.

For more detailed strategies on how to optimize your social media presence and turn followers into loyal customers, check out my book *From Likes to Profits*. It dives deep into how to choose the right social media platforms for your business to help you get the most out of each platform and convert engagement into sales.

By choosing the right platforms and developing customized strategies for each, you'll set your business up for success in the social media world. Let's make it happen!

Chapter 5: Content is King: Creating Engaging Posts That Convert

"Trustworthy content has a balanced point of view. It asks and answers the right questions. It doesn't love itself. It tries to inform and educate."

-Steve Farnsworth

When it comes to social media, content is indeed king. With so much competition for attention, the type of content you post and how you present it will determine whether your audience engages or scrolls past. But it's not just about creating any content—it's about creating posts that convert, that resonate with your audience, and that drive action. In this chapter, we'll explore the different types of content that connect with audiences, the art of storytelling, and how to balance promotional content with value-driven posts to maintain engagement.

Types of Content That Resonate

There's no one-size-fits-all when it comes to content creation, but certain types of content tend to resonate more than others. To capture your audience's attention, it's crucial to understand which formats work best on each platform and how to use them effectively. Here are four key types of content to consider:

1. **Images:** Visual content is one of the most powerful ways to capture attention. Studies show that social media posts with images get significantly higher engagement than text-only posts. Humans are naturally drawn to visuals, and the right image can communicate your brand message instantly. But not all images are created equal. High-quality, well-composed images that reflect your brand's personality are essential. Consider using images that evoke emotion, tell a story, or showcase your products or services in action.

A tip for effective use of images: **consistency is key**. Use a consistent color scheme, fonts, and style in your images to build a recognizable brand. You want your audience to instantly associate a particular aesthetic with your business.

2. Videos: Video content continues to dominate social media. With short attention spans, videos offer a dynamic way to engage your audience quickly. Whether it's a quick tutorial, a behind-the-scenes look at your business, or customer testimonials, video can help you connect with your audience on a deeper level. Live videos are another powerful tool for building relationships. They provide real-time interaction, allowing viewers to ask questions and engage with your content in a more personal way.

When creating videos, keep them **authentic and relatable**. People are less interested in polished, corporate-style videos and more drawn to real, raw, and unfiltered content that gives them a glimpse into the human side of your brand.

3. Text: While images and videos dominate social media, don't underestimate the power of well-written text posts. A compelling caption or post can engage your audience and encourage them to think, respond, and share. Text posts give you the opportunity to share insights, advice, and thought leadership that demonstrates your expertise in your field. They can also be used to inspire, ask questions, or tell stories—more on that later.

When writing text-based posts, **brevity** is your best friend. Your audience is busy and won't read a wall of text. Focus on being concise and making every word count. And don't forget to add a clear call to action (CTA), whether it's encouraging people to comment, share, or check out your latest product.

4. Stories: Social media stories (like Instagram and Facebook Stories) provide an incredible opportunity to share time-sensitive content in a more casual format. These short, temporary posts give your audience a behind-the-scenes look at your business and offer a great way to engage with them on a daily basis. Because of their temporary nature, stories are an ideal platform for announcements, sneak peeks, flash sales, and interactive content such as polls or quizzes.

The secret to a great story? **Make it interactive.** When your audience feels like they're part of your journey or decision-making process, they're more likely to stay engaged.

The Power of Storytelling: How to Weave Your Brand Story Into Your Posts

Storytelling is one of the most effective ways to create emotional connections with your audience. People don't just want to know what your business does—they want to know why you do it. They want to know your mission, your values, and your journey. This is where storytelling comes in.

Your Brand Story: Every business has a story. It could be how you started, the challenges you faced, or the passion that drives your mission. By sharing this story through your content, you create a human connection that resonates on a deeper level. Audiences are drawn to authenticity. They want to support brands that align with their values and make them feel like they're part of something bigger.

When weaving your brand story into your posts, think about the **emotions** you want to evoke. Whether it's hope, inspiration, or motivation, emotions play a crucial role in building trust and loyalty. For example, if you're a freelancer who started with nothing and built a thriving business, sharing your journey can inspire others who are in the same position. If your brand focuses on sustainability, sharing your dedication to the environment can attract like-minded customers.

Customer Stories: Another powerful way to use storytelling is by sharing your customers' stories. Social proof is one of the most persuasive forms of marketing. When your audience sees real people benefiting from your products or services, they're more likely to trust you. Testimonials, case studies, or user-generated content are excellent ways to highlight your impact while making your audience feel involved.

Consider asking satisfied customers to share their stories or even featuring them on your social media channels. When your audience sees people just like them using your products and services, they'll be more inclined to engage and convert.

Crafting Compelling Captions: Storytelling isn't limited to long-form content. A compelling caption can tell a story in just a few sentences. Start by **capturing your audience's attention** with a hook—a question, a bold statement, or a teaser that draws them in. Then, offer insight or value by sharing a story or piece of information that connects with them emotionally. Finally, end with a clear call to action that invites them to take the next step, whether that's commenting, sharing, or making a purchase.

Balancing Promotional Content with Value-Driven Posts

One of the biggest mistakes businesses make on social media is focusing too heavily on promotional content. While it's important to showcase your products and services, constantly promoting yourself can lead to disengagement. People don't want to feel like they're being sold to—they want to feel like they're gaining value from your posts.

80/20 Rule: A good rule of thumb is the 80/20 rule: 80% of your content should be focused on providing value, and 20% can be promotional. Value-driven content includes tips, advice, educational posts, or entertaining content that aligns with your brand. This content helps to build trust with your audience. When you've provided value, your audience is more likely to pay attention when you do promote your services.

For example, if you're a freelance graphic designer, you might share posts on design tips, tutorials, or industry trends. Occasionally, you can sprinkle in posts about your design packages or special offers.

Types of Value-Driven Posts

- **Educational content**: Teach your audience something new or help them solve a problem.

- **Inspirational content**: Share motivational quotes or success stories that inspire your audience to take action.

- **Interactive content**: Create polls, quizzes, or Q&A sessions that invite your audience to participate and engage.

- **Behind-the-scenes content**: Show your audience the real people behind the business. This builds connection and trust.

Call-to-Action (CTA): Even in your value-driven posts, don't be afraid to include a CTA. A well-placed CTA can lead to conversions without feeling overly promotional. For example, after sharing a useful tip, you can invite your audience to check out your blog for more insights or offer a free consultation.

Consistency is Key: The key to success on social media is consistency. By regularly posting a balanced mix of value-driven and promotional content, you'll keep your audience engaged without overwhelming them. Consistency not only builds trust but also keeps you top-of-mind when your audience is ready to make a purchase.

Action Item: Create a Content Calendar

To start implementing the strategies from this chapter, create a 30-day content calendar that includes a mix of images, videos, text, and stories. Use the 80/20 rule to ensure 80% of your posts provide value to your audience, while 20% focus on promoting your products or services.

For each post, weave in storytelling elements that reflect your brand's journey, mission, or customer success stories. Plan engaging captions with clear calls to action, and aim for consistency by posting regularly across your chosen platforms. This will help you stay organized and ensure a balanced approach to your content.

Conclusion

Creating engaging content that converts requires a thoughtful approach. By understanding what types of content resonate with your audience, harnessing the power of storytelling, and balancing promotional and value-driven posts, you can build a loyal and engaged following. Remember, social media is a long game. With patience, persistence, and a focus on providing value, your content will start driving conversions and contributing to the success of your business.

Chapter 6: Building an Engaged Community

"Engage, Enlighten, Encourage and especially...just be yourself! Social media is a community effort, everyone is an asset."

-Susan Cooper

In today's fast-paced digital world, having followers is not enough. Sure, numbers matter when it comes to visibility, but what truly propels a business forward is building an engaged community. The difference between a passive audience and an interactive one can mean the difference between surviving and thriving in your business. If you want to create a lasting impact, focus on fostering genuine connections rather than just chasing follower counts. Your goal should be to cultivate a community that believes in your brand, shares your vision, and is eager to engage with what you have to offer. So how do you build an engaged community that lasts? Let's dive into it.

The Difference Between Followers and an Engaged Community

At first glance, it may seem like followers and an engaged community are the same thing. After all, your followers are part of your audience. But here's the truth: not all followers are created equal. Some may scroll past your posts without a second glance, while others may actively engage, comment, share, and support your content. The key is recognizing that followers are simply people who hit the follow button, but an engaged community consists of individuals who feel personally invested in your brand.

Followers: Numbers vs. Connection

When you're focused solely on building followers, your priority may shift toward vanity metrics—how many people clicked "like" or how large your audience has grown. But are those numbers actually converting into meaningful connections? Often, people chase these numbers for the wrong reasons, thinking that a high follower count is the ultimate goal. While it might offer a quick ego boost, large numbers without genuine engagement mean very little in the grand scheme of things.

In contrast, an engaged community consists of individuals who not only follow you but also interact with your content. These people find value in your message and take the time to contribute to the conversation, share their thoughts, ask questions, and even advocate for your brand. They are not just passive spectators but active participants. When you nurture this kind of audience, they become loyal fans who are more likely to support your business, recommend you to others, and help you grow organically.

Tips for Encouraging Interaction and Two-Way Communication

Building an engaged community doesn't happen overnight. It requires consistency, authenticity, and the willingness to create spaces for dialogue. Here are some tips to help you foster interaction and two-way communication with your audience:

1. Be Authentic and Transparent

People gravitate toward authenticity. They can tell when you're being real and when you're putting on a front. Share your journey, your struggles, and your victories with honesty. When you open up to your audience, it creates a space for them to do the same. Remember, people engage with people—not brands or faceless corporations. Let your personality shine through in your content, and encourage your community to share their experiences as well.

2. Ask Open-Ended Questions

If you want people to engage, give them something to talk about. Asking open-ended questions is one of the simplest yet most effective ways to spark conversation. Whether you're posting on social media, sending out an email newsletter, or engaging on your blog, encourage your audience to share their thoughts by posing questions that require more than just a yes or no answer.

Example: Instead of asking, "Did you like our latest post?" ask, "What was your biggest takeaway from our latest post, and how are you going to apply it in your life?"

3. Respond to Comments and Messages

Communication is a two-way street. If your audience takes the time to comment on your post or send you a message, don't leave them hanging. Responding to comments and messages shows that you value your audience's input and care about what they have to say. This helps foster a sense of connection and trust. Plus, when people see that you're active and responsive, they'll be more likely to engage with your content in the future.

4. Create Engaging Content

If you want people to interact, your content needs to give them a reason to do so. Focus on creating posts that are not only informative but also entertaining and emotionally engaging. Use storytelling, humor, or inspiring messages to evoke a reaction. Create polls, quizzes, or interactive stories that allow your audience to participate actively. Make sure to mix up your content to keep things fresh and exciting.

5. Host Live Events or Q&A Sessions

Nothing sparks engagement like real-time interaction. Hosting live events—whether it's a Q&A session, a webinar, or a behind-the-scenes tour—offers your audience an opportunity to engage with you directly. People love having a space where they can ask questions in real time, hear your thoughts, and feel connected to the person behind the brand.

6. Give Shoutouts and Acknowledge Your Community

Recognizing the individuals who actively engage with your content goes a long way in building community loyalty. Give shoutouts to loyal followers or customers, highlight user-generated content, and show appreciation for the support they give. When people feel seen and appreciated, they're more likely to continue engaging and even recommend your brand to others.

How to Nurture Relationships with Your Audience to Create Loyal Fans

Building an engaged community is the first step, but nurturing those relationships is what will turn casual followers into loyal fans. Here's how you can deepen your connection with your audience over time:

1. Consistency is Key

Consistency in how you show up for your community is crucial to building long-lasting relationships. Whether it's regular posts, blog updates, or email newsletters, stick to a schedule that your audience can rely on. Over time, this builds trust. When people know they can count on you to consistently deliver value, they'll stick around and become more invested in your brand.

2. Personalize Your Approach

Treat your audience members like individuals, not numbers. Personalizing your communication—whether through personalized email campaigns, addressing people by name in comments, or referring to previous interactions—helps build deeper connections. People appreciate when they feel like they're part of an inner circle rather than just another follower in the crowd.

3. Provide Value Without Expecting Immediate Returns

Offer valuable content, advice, or resources without always asking for something in return. Your audience needs to know that you're there to serve them, not just sell to them. When you provide value consistently—whether it's tips, insights, or inspiration—your community will grow more loyal because they see you as a trusted resource.

4. Be Vulnerable and Show Humility

People relate to those who are real and not afraid to admit their flaws. When you share your own struggles, setbacks, and lessons learned, your audience will connect with you on a deeper level. This vulnerability helps humanize your brand and fosters a sense of community because people feel they can relate to you.

5. Offer Exclusive Perks to Your Community

One of the ways to nurture loyal fans is by giving them access to exclusive content, offers, or experiences that others don't have. Whether it's early access to new products, discounts, behind-the-scenes content, or private group memberships, offering perks creates a sense of belonging and makes your community feel special.

Action Item: Build Your Engaged Community

1. **Start a Conversation:** This week, post something on your social media platform of choice that invites your audience to share their thoughts. It could be an open-ended question, a poll, or a request for feedback.

2. **Respond with Intention:** Over the next few days, make an intentional effort to reply to comments, messages, or emails from your audience. Let them know you value their input.

3. **Plan a Live Event:** Choose a date within the next month to host a live Q&A, workshop, or webinar for your community. Use it as an opportunity to engage with your audience in real time and deepen your connection with them.

4. **Personalize Communication:** Over the next week, identify a few key members of your community who regularly engage with your content. Send them a personalized message thanking them for their support, and make it clear you appreciate their contributions.

Building an engaged community takes time, effort, and authenticity. But when you focus on creating real connections, providing value, and nurturing relationships, you'll find that your audience isn't just following you—they're rooting for you. And that's when the magic happens.

Chapter 7: Social Media Growth Strategies

"Content is fire, social media is gasoline."

-Ryan Kahn

In today's digital landscape, social media is more than just a platform for sharing moments; it's a powerful tool for building a thriving business and community. Whether you're a freelancer, a small business owner, or a content creator, social media can be the key that unlocks your next level of success. But growing on social media takes more than just posting regularly—it requires strategy, authenticity, and a deep understanding of your audience.

When done right, social media growth can help you connect with your ideal audience, amplify your message, and create a loyal community of raving fans. So, how can you tap into that potential? Let's dive into some key strategies that will not only increase your social media following but also deepen your engagement and connection with those who follow you.

6 Social Media Strategies to Start You On Your Way:

1. Know Your Audience: Create Content that Resonates

Before you can grow, you need to know who you're growing with. It's easy to get caught up in the number of followers, but the real power lies in knowing your audience deeply. Who are they? What do they care about? What problems are they trying to solve?

Take time to really understand the needs and desires of your audience. What are they searching for on social media? What kind of content excites or inspires them? When you can answer these questions, you can create content that speaks directly to them—content that they not only want to engage with but also share with others.

The key here is relevance. The more your audience sees themselves in your content, the more likely they are to interact with it and help your message spread. Whether it's through polls, questions, stories, or comments, find ways to continually ask your audience what they need. Listen to their feedback and adjust your content accordingly. Your goal should be to create content that adds value to their lives, making them feel seen and understood.

2. Leverage the Power of Storytelling

Storytelling is the heart of social media growth. People don't just want to follow brands or businesses—they want to connect with stories. They want to feel like they are part of something bigger than themselves.

Your story, your mission, and the journey you're on can inspire your audience. By sharing behind-the-scenes moments, personal challenges, or victories, you humanize your brand and create a sense of connection. Storytelling fosters trust and loyalty, which is the foundation of any thriving community.

Remember, your audience isn't just interested in what you offer—they're interested in *why* you do it. Use your social media posts to share the deeper "why" behind your business or brand. Tell stories that reflect your values and vision. Use your captions, videos, and live streams as a canvas for your authentic voice.

In addition to sharing your own story, share the stories of your community members or customers. Testimonials, user-generated content, and success stories are powerful tools for growth. When others see themselves in the stories you share, they'll be drawn to engage with you on a deeper level.

3. Engage, Don't Just Broadcast

Too many people treat social media like a one-way megaphone—constantly broadcasting but never listening. True growth happens when you shift your mindset from broadcasting to engaging.

Social media is called "social" for a reason. It's meant to be a conversation, not a monologue. Engage with your followers by responding to comments, liking their posts, and replying to their messages. This shows that you care about them as individuals, not just as numbers. The more personal and interactive you are, the more your audience will feel valued and stick around.

Engagement is a two-way street. Not only should you respond to your audience, but you should also initiate conversations. Ask questions, run polls, and encourage your followers to share their thoughts. Create content that invites interaction—whether it's through live streams, stories, or discussion threads. The more engagement you spark, the more your posts will be seen by a wider audience thanks to social media algorithms.

Think of your social media platforms as a community space, not just a billboard. The stronger your engagement, the more your audience will grow, and the deeper your connection with your followers will become.

4. Consistency is Key

Growing your social media presence isn't an overnight process. It takes time, patience, and most importantly, consistency. Showing up regularly is essential if you want to build trust with your audience.

That doesn't mean you have to post every day, but it does mean you should create a schedule that you can stick to. Whether it's three times a week or every day, commit to posting consistently. This helps your audience know when to expect new content from you and keeps your brand top-of-mind.

In addition to consistency in frequency, aim for consistency in your brand voice, tone, and aesthetic. Your followers should have a cohesive experience when they engage with your content across platforms. Consistency builds recognition and trust, both of which are crucial for growth.

Remember, consistency isn't just about the number of posts—it's about showing up with value. Make sure each post contributes to your overall mission and delivers something meaningful to your audience.

5. Collaborate with Others

One of the fastest ways to grow on social media is through collaboration. Partnering with others who share a similar audience can introduce you to new followers and expand your reach. Whether it's through guest posts, joint live streams, interviews, or shout-outs, collaboration helps you tap into new communities while building valuable relationships.

Look for opportunities to collaborate with influencers, brands, or other creators who align with your values. Collaborations allow you to leverage each other's strengths and audiences, creating a win-win situation for everyone involved.

When collaborating, always keep the focus on creating value for your combined audience. Authentic partnerships that benefit both parties and their followers are far more effective than one-off promotions or superficial shout-outs.

6. Embrace Video Content

Video is the king of content when it comes to social media growth. Whether it's TikTok, Instagram Reels, YouTube, or live streams, video content captures attention in ways that static posts simply can't.

The great thing about video is that it allows you to connect with your audience on a more personal level. It brings your brand to life and gives your audience a chance to see the person behind the posts. Whether you're giving tutorials, sharing insights, or going behind the scenes, video content creates a sense of immediacy and authenticity.

If you're not already using video in your social media strategy, now is the time to start. You don't need professional equipment or fancy editing—what matters most is the value you provide. Experiment with different video formats, from quick tips to longer deep dives, and see what resonates most with your audience.

Action Items: Grow Your Social Media Today

1. **Create a Content Plan for the Next 30 Days:** Plan your posts, stories, and videos for the next month. Make sure to include a mix of valuable content, personal storytelling, and engagement-driven posts.

2. **Set a Goal for Engagement:** Commit to engaging with at least 10 of your followers each day. Like, comment, and reply to their content to start building stronger connections.

3. **Record and Share One Video This Week:** Whether it's a short story, a reel, or a live stream, challenge yourself to create and post one video. Focus on connecting authentically with your audience.

4. **Find a Collaboration Partner:** Identify someone whose audience aligns with yours and brainstorm how you can collaborate in a way that provides value to both of your followers.

5. **Track What Works:** Review your analytics regularly to see what kind of content gets the most engagement. Use this data to adjust your content strategy moving forward.

Social media growth doesn't have to feel overwhelming. With the right strategies and consistent action, you can create a thriving online community that supports your mission and goals. Remember, it's not about the numbers—it's about connection, authenticity, and adding value. When you lead with that, the growth will follow. Keep showing up, keep engaging, and watch your community thrive!

Chapter 8: Leveraging User-GeneratedContent and Social Proof

"People tend to believe in user-generated content more than advertisements because it's less likely to mislead or misinform in the eyes of the consumer."

-Chris Starkhagen

When it comes to the ever-evolving world of social media, where countless brands and businesses are competing for attention, one thing remains constant: people trust people more than they trust brands. This is why **user-generated content (UGC)** and **social proof** are such powerful tools for building a thriving online community and fostering loyalty. Leveraging these strategies not only validates your business but also encourages your followers to become active participants in your brand's journey.

Let's explore how UGC and social proof can amplify your social media presence, engage your audience, and inspire them to take action. We'll also dive into practical ways you can start incorporating these powerful tools into your strategy today.

What is User-Generated Content (UGC)?

User-generated content is any form of content—photos, videos, reviews, testimonials, blog posts, or social media posts—created by your customers or community members rather than your brand. It's authentic, organic, and speaks directly to the experiences of real people interacting with your product or service. This type of content can often have a much bigger impact than any professional ad campaign you run.

When people share their own experiences with your brand, they are essentially endorsing you to their friends, family, and followers. And there's no stronger form of marketing than word of mouth. UGC helps potential customers visualize themselves using your product, feeling the benefits, and becoming part of your community.

Why Social Proof Matters

At its core, social proof is the concept that people tend to follow the actions of others when they are uncertain about a decision. In other words, when someone sees that a product or service is popular or trusted by others, they are more likely to try it themselves. Social proof comes in many forms, including:

- **Testimonials** from happy customers
- **Reviews** and **ratings** on platforms like Amazon, Google, or Yelp
- **Shout-outs** and mentions from influencers or industry experts
- **Case studies** showing how your product helped solve a problem
- The number of **followers**, **likes**, or **comments** you receive on social media

Social proof serves as validation for potential customers that your brand delivers on its promises. When they see others having positive experiences with your products, it reduces any perceived risk and builds trust.

The Power of Authenticity

One of the biggest advantages of UGC and social proof is their authenticity. In a world where consumers are increasingly skeptical of overly polished ads, real content from real people cuts through the noise.

A photo of a customer using your product in their everyday life can have a far greater impact than a highly produced marketing image. Why? Because it feels genuine. It shows potential customers that people just like them are benefiting from what you offer. This kind of authenticity is priceless in today's digital marketing landscape.

For example, a fitness brand might share photos of everyday customers achieving their fitness goals using their products, rather than only featuring professional athletes in promotional materials. This helps potential customers feel like the brand is accessible and attainable, no matter where they are on their fitness journey.

Building Community Through UGC

When you encourage your followers to create content, you are giving them a voice in your brand's story. This transforms them from passive consumers into active participants in your community. And when people feel involved in something, they're more likely to stay engaged and loyal.

Encouraging UGC can take many forms, such as:

- **Running a contest or challenge**: Invite your followers to share photos or videos of them using your product, and offer a prize for the most creative or inspiring entry.

- **Creating a branded hashtag**: Encourage customers to use a specific hashtag when they share content related to your brand. This not only makes it easy to find and share their content, but it also helps build a sense of community around the hashtag.

- **Featuring user content on your page**: When you share UGC on your own social media or website, you're showing your customers that you value their experiences and contributions. This simple act can go a long way in strengthening the bond between you and your community.

For example, Starbucks is known for running seasonal hashtag campaigns where they invite customers to share pictures of their customized drinks using specific hashtags. Not only does this flood social media with content about their products, but it also gives their customers a fun way to express their individuality.

How to Encourage UGC

Not all customers will automatically share their experiences with your brand, so you need to actively encourage UGC. Here are a few ways you can do this:

1. **Ask for It**: Sometimes, all you need to do is ask. Include a call to action in your posts, emails, or product packaging that encourages customers to share their experiences on social media. Offer incentives, such as the chance to be featured on your page or win a giveaway.

2. **Make It Easy**: The easier you make it for your customers to share, the more likely they are to do it. Provide clear instructions on how to tag your brand or use a specific hashtag, and make sure your social media accounts are easy to find.

3. **Offer Incentives**: People love rewards, so consider offering a discount, free product, or entry into a giveaway in exchange for UGC. Just be sure the offer is aligned with your brand and doesn't feel forced.

4. **Engage with the Content**: When customers share content featuring your brand, show them some love! Like, comment, and share their posts. This not only boosts your engagement but also encourages others to share their experiences.

Using Social Proof to Build Trust

In addition to UGC, social proof can come from reviews, testimonials, and endorsements. Here are some ways you can leverage social proof to boost your brand's credibility:

1. **Share Customer Testimonials**: Ask your customers for testimonials and feature them on your website and social media. These can be in the form of written quotes, videos, or even screenshots of positive comments.

2. **Highlight Positive Reviews**: If your product or service is listed on review sites, make sure to regularly check and share positive reviews. You can even create a "Review of the Week" feature to spotlight particularly glowing feedback.

3. **Showcase Endorsements**: If you've been featured by an influencer, blogger, or

media outlet, share these endorsements widely. When people see that trusted figures are endorsing your brand, they're more likely to follow suit.

4. **Use Numbers**: Sometimes, the numbers speak for themselves. If you've reached a milestone, such as selling 10,000 units or having 1,000 five-star reviews, share that information with your audience as social proof that your brand is thriving.

Case Study: Glossier's UGC Success

Glossier, the beauty brand, has built its entire marketing strategy around UGC and social proof. From the very beginning, they've relied on their customers to create content showcasing how they use and love Glossier products. They've even built their brand identity around the idea that beauty is personal and that their products are for real people, not just models.

By encouraging their customers to share their experiences and reposting UGC on their social media accounts, Glossier has created a massive community of engaged followers who feel like they're part of the brand. This approach has helped them grow organically, with minimal spending on traditional advertising.

Action Items: Leverage UGC and Social Proof Today

1. **Create a Branded Hashtag:** Develop a unique hashtag for your brand and encourage your followers to use it when they share content related to your products. Promote the hashtag in your bio, posts, and emails.

2. **Run a UGC Contest:** Launch a contest where customers share photos or videos of them using your product. Offer a prize for the best entry, and feature the winner on your social media.

3. **Ask for Reviews and Testimonials:** Reach out to your happiest customers and ask them to leave a review or provide a testimonial. Share these across your social media and website.

4. **Engage with UGC:** Make it a habit to like, comment on, and share user-generated content. Show your customers that you appreciate them, and encourage

others to do the same.

5. **Leverage Numbers for Social Proof:** If you've hit a significant milestone, such as a certain number of followers, reviews, or sales, share this information as a form of social proof. Let your audience know that others are loving your product or service.

By incorporating user-generated content and social proof into your social media strategy, you not only build trust but also foster a sense of community. Remember, people trust real people, and when you let your customers share their stories, your brand grows organically and authentically. So, get ready to watch your community thrive by harnessing the power of your audience's voice!

Chapter 9: Managing and Automating Your Social Media

"The first rule of social media is that everything changes all the time. What won't change is the community's desire to network."

-Kami Huyse

As entrepreneurs, small business owners, and freelancers, it often feels like there aren't enough hours in the day to tackle everything on your to-do list. Between creating content, engaging with followers, and analyzing performance, managing your social media can quickly become overwhelming. This is where automation steps in as a game changer.

Social media automation is the key to staying consistent, efficient, and effective. It allows you to focus on what matters most—engaging with your community and growing your business. It's about working smarter, not harder, and using tools that help streamline your tasks without losing the human touch.

In this chapter, we'll explore how to manage your social media more effectively by automating repetitive tasks while still maintaining an authentic connection with your audience. You'll also learn practical tips and strategies that will free up your time and energy for the creative aspects of your business.

Why Social Media Management Matters

Effective social media management is the backbone of a thriving online presence. Posting sporadically or inconsistently can cause your audience to lose interest, while haphazard engagement leads to missed opportunities. If you want to see real results, you need to approach social media with the same level of care and strategy that you would with any other part of your business.

A well-managed social media presence helps you:

- **Build trust** with your audience by showing up consistently.

- **Engage** with your community in meaningful ways.

- **Grow your reach** through regular, quality content.

- **Save time** by planning and automating repetitive tasks.

By developing a strategy and utilizing automation tools, you can take control of your social media in a way that feels less like a chore and more like an integral part of your business growth.

The Benefits of Social Media Automation

When used wisely, social media automation can have profound effects on your business. It enables you to:

1. **Save Time:** Scheduling posts in advance allows you to batch your content creation and focus on other areas of your business.

2. **Maintain Consistency:** Automation ensures that you maintain a steady presence on social media, even during busy periods or vacations.

3. **Reduce Stress:** Knowing your posts are planned and scheduled takes the pressure off needing to come up with last-minute content.

4. **Improve Engagement:** Automation doesn't mean detachment. With more time freed up, you can dedicate your energy to meaningful engagement with your audience.

5. **Analyze and Refine Your Strategy:** Many automation tools provide detailed analytics that help you understand what's working and what's not, so you can continuously improve your strategy.

Tools for Automating Your Social Media

There are a variety of tools that can help automate different aspects of your social media management, from scheduling posts to analyzing performance. Here are a few examples of popular automation tools:

1. **Hootsuite:** One of the most widely used tools, Hootsuite allows you to schedule posts across multiple platforms, monitor mentions, and engage with your audience, all from one dashboard. Hootsuite is pretty expensive though they do have a free 30-day trial so you can see if it fits your business.

2. **Buffer:** Another scheduling tool that simplifies social media management by allowing you to plan, schedule, and analyze content performance across all major platforms. I currently use Buffer because I like the platform and they do offer a free plan that allows you to connect up to 3 social media platforms. It does have limitations as far as how many posts you can schedule on that free plan but I used the free plan for years. I only recently upgraded to their Essential plan which is $180 per year.

3. **Later:** A visual-first platform that's perfect for Instagram and Pinterest, Later allows you to plan and schedule posts while focusing on aesthetics and visuals. They do have a free plan as well as several paid plans.

4. **Sprout Social:** A more advanced platform that combines scheduling, analytics, and engagement features, helping you manage every aspect of your social media presence. I used Sprout Social for a little while when I worked at a digital agency as a social media manager but haven't used it since. I believe it's a little more than what's needed for most small or freelance businesses and it is quite expensive.

What Should You Automate?

While automation is incredibly helpful, it's essential to find the right balance between what you automate and where you remain hands-on. Here are a few areas where automation can make a significant impact:

1. **Content Scheduling:** Automating your posts across platforms is one of the easiest ways to save time. You can batch-create content and schedule it to go out at the optimal times for your audience. This ensures that you're always staying top of mind without the daily effort.

2. **Content Curation:** Automating content curation allows you to share relevant articles, blogs, or industry news with your followers without manually searching for them. Tools like Pocket or Feedly can help you gather content based on your niche, and you can schedule it for sharing.

3. **Monitoring and Alerts:** Automation tools can notify you when your brand is mentioned online, so you can respond promptly. This is especially useful for customer service or reputation management.

4. **Reporting and Analytics:** Tracking performance can be time-consuming, but with the right tools, you can automate reporting. Tools like Sprout Social or Buffer provide detailed analytics, allowing you to review what's working and make data-driven decisions for future content.

What Should You Not Automate?

While automation can be incredibly beneficial, not everything should be automated. Authenticity and personal interaction are crucial to building a strong community, so make sure you stay personally involved in the following areas:

1. **Engagement and Responses:** Your audience wants to connect with you, not a bot. Automated responses can feel cold and impersonal, so make sure you're taking the time to respond to comments, messages, and questions directly.

2. **Live Content:** Platforms like Instagram Stories, Facebook Live, and TikTok thrive on real-time interaction. Authentic live content shows your audience the human side of your brand, and this is something that cannot be replicated through automation.

3. **Creative Content Development:** While automation can help with scheduling, the creative process behind developing meaningful and engaging content should always be hands-on. This is your opportunity to share your brand's voice and vision.

Maintaining the Human Touch in Automation

It's important to remember that automation should enhance your efforts, not replace the personal touch. Your followers are looking for real connections, so while automation takes care of the logistical aspects, you should focus on providing the human element.

Here are a few ways to maintain the human touch even with automation:

1. **Personalize Your Content:** Even when you automate posts, make sure your content speaks directly to your audience. Use language and visuals that resonate with them on a personal level.

2. **Engage with Your Community:** Schedule time each day to respond to comments, answer questions, and join conversations. This is where relationships are built.

3. **Mix Automated Posts with Live Content:** Balance your scheduled posts with real-time updates. This can include Instagram Stories, live streams, or impromptu behind-the-scenes content.

4. **Monitor Trends and Adjust:** Use automation to your advantage by automating your content, but stay nimble enough to adjust to trends or current events. If something big happens in your industry or the world, make sure your content reflects that.

Case Study: Automating for Success

Consider the success of **Entrepreneur Magazine** on social media. Their team uses tools like Hootsuite to schedule their regular content, ensuring they have a consistent flow of articles, insights, and tips posted across platforms. By automating the posting process, they can focus on creating high-quality content and engaging directly with their community. They also use automation to track performance metrics, allowing them to refine their strategy based on real-time data.

By automating the repetitive tasks, Entrepreneur is able to invest more time into delivering value to their audience, resulting in higher engagement and stronger connections with their community.

Action Items: Automate and Manage Your Social Media Efficiently

1. **Choose an Automation Tool:** Pick one or more tools like Hootsuite, Buffer, or Sprout Social that align with your business needs. Start with scheduling posts for one week at a time and gradually work up to scheduling an entire month.

2. **Batch Create Content:** Dedicate time each week to create and schedule content in batches. This will allow you to focus on other aspects of your business without worrying about daily posting.

3. **Automate Monitoring:** Use tools like Google Alerts or Sprout Social to set up notifications for when your brand is mentioned online. Respond promptly to maintain a strong relationship with your audience.

4. **Set Aside Time for Engagement:** Automate your content, but stay engaged with your community. Schedule daily or weekly time blocks for interacting with comments, responding to DMs, and staying active in conversations.

5. **Analyze Your Performance:** Use the reporting and analytics features of your automation tool to evaluate the success of your content. Pay attention to which posts receive the most engagement and adjust your strategy based on the data.

By managing and automating your social media, you are taking a proactive step toward maintaining a strong online presence while freeing up your time for other important aspects of your business. The right balance of automation and personal engagement will allow you to grow your community authentically, stay consistent, and build lasting relationships with your audience.

Chapter 10: Analyzing and Measuring Success

"You are responsible for everything you post and everything you post will become a reflection of you."

-Germany Kent

In the fast-paced world of social media, it's easy to get swept up in the constant need to create content and engage with your audience. But how do you know if all that effort is truly paying off? That's where analyzing and measuring your success comes in. It's not enough to just post and hope for the best—you need to track your progress, assess what's working, and refine your strategy to maximize your results.

Analyzing your success on social media is like steering a ship. Without knowing where you're headed or how you're performing, you risk drifting off course. But with the right tools and strategies in place, you can chart a course toward growth, engagement, and thriving online communities.

In this chapter, we'll dive into how to measure your social media success, what key metrics to focus on, and how to use that data to make informed decisions for your business. Remember, success isn't a one-time achievement—it's a journey that requires ongoing attention, reflection, and adjustment.

Why Measuring Success Matters

When it comes to social media, success can mean different things depending on your goals. Whether you're aiming for increased brand awareness, engagement with your audience, lead generation, or conversion to sales, understanding the effectiveness of your efforts is critical.

Measuring success allows you to:

- **Track Growth:** Understand how your audience is growing over time and how your content is resonating with them.

- **Refine Strategy:** Identify what's working and what's not, so you can focus on the content that drives the best results.

- **Allocate Resources:** Know where to invest your time, energy, and budget to achieve maximum impact.

- **Celebrate Wins:** Acknowledge and appreciate milestones in your journey, which helps keep you motivated and aligned with your long-term vision.

Without a clear understanding of your progress, you're essentially navigating in the dark. Tracking and analyzing your social media performance ensures you're moving in the right direction and continuously improving.

What Should You Measure? Key Metrics for Success

Success on social media is multi-dimensional, and there are a variety of metrics that can help you measure different aspects of your performance. Here are some of the key metrics to focus on:

1. Engagement Rate

Engagement rate measures how actively your audience is interacting with your content. This includes likes, comments, shares, and clicks. A high engagement rate indicates that your content resonates with your audience and prompts them to take action.

- **How to Calculate Engagement Rate:** Engagement rate = (Total Engagements / Total Impressions or Followers) x 100

For example, if a post received 150 likes, 30 comments, and 20 shares, with a total of 10,000 impressions, your engagement rate would be 2%—a great benchmark depending on your platform and industry.

2. Follower Growth

Tracking follower growth over time helps you understand how your audience is expanding. This metric is particularly important if one of your goals is to increase brand awareness.

- **Pro Tip:** Don't just focus on the numbers—pay attention to the quality of followers. Are they engaging with your content? Are they aligned with your target audience?

3. Website Traffic

If you're using social media to drive traffic to your website or blog, this is an essential metric to measure. Tools like Google Analytics allow you to see how much traffic is coming from social media, which platforms are most effective, and which posts or campaigns drive the most visitors.

- **Example:** Let's say you posted a product feature on Instagram with a link to your website. By tracking how many visitors came from that post, you can gauge the success of your campaign.

4. Conversion Rate

Conversion rate refers to the percentage of social media visitors who take a desired action, such as signing up for a newsletter, purchasing a product, or downloading a free resource.

- **How to Calculate Conversion Rate:** Conversion rate = (Total Conversions / Total Clicks) x 100

This is one of the most important metrics for businesses looking to generate leads or sales through social media. It allows you to measure the effectiveness of your social media efforts in driving meaningful actions.

5. Reach and Impressions

Reach refers to the total number of unique users who have seen your content, while impressions represent the total number of times your content has been displayed (including multiple views by the same user). Monitoring these metrics helps you understand the visibility of your content and whether it's being widely seen.

- **Example:** If a Facebook post has 5,000 impressions but only reaches 3,000 users, it means some users saw your post multiple times. This might indicate the content is popular or being shared.

6. Return on Investment (ROI)

If you're running paid social media campaigns, it's essential to measure the return on investment (ROI). This metric helps you understand how much revenue is generated compared to the amount spent on ads or promotions.

- **How to Calculate ROI:** ROI = (Revenue − Cost of Investment) / Cost of Investment

If you spent $200 on Facebook ads and generated $600 in sales, your ROI would be 2x, meaning you made twice your investment back.

Tools for Measuring Success

To effectively track and analyze these metrics, you need the right tools in place. Fortunately, there are numerous platforms designed to help you gather data and insights:

- **Google Analytics:** Ideal for tracking website traffic and conversions from social media.

- **Sprout Social:** A robust tool that provides detailed reports on engagement, follower growth, and content performance.

- **Hootsuite Analytics:** Offers insights into reach, impressions, and engagement across multiple social platforms.

- **Facebook Insights:** Built-in analytics tool for tracking the performance of your posts, page, and ads on Facebook.

- **Instagram Insights:** A great tool for tracking engagement and follower demographics on Instagram.

These tools help you make sense of your data so that you can optimize your strategy for better results.

How to Use Your Data to Improve

Collecting data is only the first step; the real magic happens when you use that data to improve your social media efforts. Here's how to do it:

1. **Identify What's Working:** Look at your top-performing posts in terms of engagement, reach, and conversions. What made these posts successful? Was it the type of content, the timing, or the platform?

2. **Pinpoint What's Not:** Just as important as identifying successes is figuring out what isn't resonating with your audience. Review posts with low engagement or high reach but low conversions. Could the content be more targeted, or do you need to adjust your call-to-action?

3. **Adjust Your Strategy:** Based on the data, refine your strategy to focus on what's driving the most results. For example, if you notice that posts with infographics receive the most shares, consider creating more of that type of content.

4. **Test and Experiment:** Social media success is all about experimenting. Try posting at different times, testing new content formats, or even running A/B tests on your paid ads to see what works best.

Examples of Measuring Success

Let's look at an example. Imagine a small business owner, Sarah, runs an online boutique. She uses Instagram and Facebook to market her products. Sarah sets a goal of increasing website traffic and generating sales from her social media efforts.

1. **After running a series of product posts on Instagram,** Sarah checks her Instagram Insights and sees that her engagement rate has increased, with more likes and comments than usual. This is a great sign that her content resonates

with her audience.

2. **Next, she looks at her Google Analytics data** and sees that traffic to her website from Instagram has doubled. However, conversions (purchases) remain low. Sarah decides to refine her strategy by adding a more direct call-to-action in her posts and offering a discount code for her Instagram followers.

3. **Two weeks later,** Sarah measures her data again and notices that not only has her traffic increased, but her conversion rate has also jumped from 1.5% to 3%. This tells her that the adjustments she made were effective in turning engagement into sales.

Action Items: Analyzing and Measuring Success

1. **Set Clear Goals:** Before diving into the data, set clear goals for what you want to achieve. Are you looking to increase engagement, drive website traffic, or generate more sales? These goals will determine which metrics to focus on.

2. **Choose the Right Tools:** Select tools like Google Analytics, Sprout Social, or Hootsuite to track your performance. Set them up to monitor key metrics such as engagement rate, follower growth, and website conversions.

3. **Review Your Metrics Weekly:** Dedicate time each week to reviewing your metrics. Look for patterns in what's working and what's not, and identify areas where you can improve. Consistency is key.

4. **Test and Adjust Your Strategy:** Use your data to refine your strategy. Experiment with different content types, posting times, and engagement tactics to see what works best for your audience.

5. **Celebrate Your Wins:** Don't forget to celebrate your progress! Whether it's a boost in followers, an increase in engagement, or hitting a conversion milestone, acknowledging your wins keeps you motivated on your social media journey.

Measuring your social media success is the key to growth. By tracking the right metrics, using data-driven insights to refine your strategy, and celebrating your progress, you'll build a thriving, engaged community. Success on social media doesn't happen overnight, but with patience, persistence, and purposeful adjustments, you'll continue to see incredible results. Keep going, and remember: every bit of data is a stepping stone to greater impact!

Chapter 11: Handling Negative Feedback and Online Crises

"If you make customers unhappy in the physical world, they might each tell 6 friends. If you make customers unhappy on the internet, they can each tell 6,000 friends."

-Jeff Bezos

In the world of social media, not every comment will be filled with praise, and not every interaction will go as planned. Negative feedback, critical comments, and even full-blown online crises are part of the reality of engaging with the public. But here's the key: it's not about avoiding criticism—it's about handling it with grace, resilience, and turning challenges into opportunities for growth.

Negative feedback can feel overwhelming, especially when you've poured your heart into your business, products, or services. But these situations often hold the potential for learning, improvement, and even deepening the trust of your community. What defines your social media success isn't whether or not you receive negative feedback, but how you respond to it.

This chapter will explore strategies for effectively handling negative feedback and managing online crises, helping you maintain your credibility and foster a positive, resilient community. We'll cover how to navigate criticism with professionalism, address online crises with clarity, and come out stronger on the other side.

The Nature of Negative Feedback: An Opportunity for Growth

No matter how great your product or service is, you're bound to encounter negative feedback at some point. It's a natural part of being visible online. The good news is that negative feedback can often provide valuable insights into areas where you can improve.

Example 1: Addressing Product Criticism

Imagine you run a small business that sells eco-friendly skincare products. One day, you receive a comment on Instagram from a customer claiming your moisturizer caused irritation. Your initial reaction may be frustration or defensiveness, but this is a golden opportunity to show transparency and care.

How to Handle It: Respond with empathy, acknowledge their experience, and offer a solution. A simple reply like, "We're so sorry to hear that! Everyone's skin is unique, and we appreciate your feedback. We'd love to chat more and see how we can help. Please send us a DM so we can resolve this together." This shows that you care about your customers' well-being and are willing to make things right.

Outcome: Not only have you addressed the negative feedback, but you've also showcased your commitment to customer service in a public space. Others who see this interaction will trust your brand even more because you handled criticism professionally and with empathy.

Example 2: Dealing with Service Complaints

Let's say you're a freelance graphic designer and a client leaves a negative review on your Facebook page, claiming you missed a deadline. While your instinct may be to defend your reputation, it's crucial to address this complaint without appearing defensive.

How to Handle It: Acknowledge their frustration, take responsibility if applicable, and offer a path forward. For example, "Thank you for your feedback. We understand how important timelines are, and we sincerely apologize for the delay. We'd love to connect with you privately to discuss how we can improve your experience moving forward."

Outcome: By responding calmly and taking ownership, you demonstrate professionalism and integrity. Even if the original commenter doesn't respond positively, others observing the interaction will respect how you handled it.

Managing Online Crises: Stay Calm and Be Proactive

An online crisis can arise in many forms—whether it's a viral negative comment, a public relations misstep, or even a coordinated effort by disgruntled customers. How you manage an online crisis can define your brand for years to come.

Step 1: Assess the Situation

When an online crisis strikes, the first step is to pause and assess the situation. Is this an isolated incident, or are multiple people involved? Is the issue factual, or is it based on misunderstanding or misinformation? Gathering the facts helps you form a clear and strategic response.

- **Example:** A local restaurant faced backlash after a customer posted a video claiming they found a foreign object in their meal. Before responding publicly, the restaurant reviewed its security footage, spoke with the customer privately, and gathered information from staff. By being thorough in their assessment, they were able to address the situation factually, and in a way that demonstrated responsibility.

Step 2: Take Responsibility When Necessary

If the crisis stems from a legitimate mistake made by your business, take responsibility. Owning up to your errors builds trust and credibility. People are generally forgiving when they see a brand acknowledge a mistake and take action to correct it.

- **Example:** A clothing brand released a controversial ad campaign that was deemed offensive by some customers. The brand immediately pulled the campaign, issued a public apology, and outlined specific steps they were taking to ensure this wouldn't happen again. Their swift response and accountability helped them regain the trust of their audience.

Step 3: Communicate Transparently

In times of crisis, people want to know what's happening and how you're handling the situation. Communicate clearly and transparently, addressing concerns directly. Silence can often make a situation worse, leading people to speculate or assume the worst.

- **Example:** During a product recall, a fitness equipment company regularly updated its social media followers with information on how to return the product and what steps they were taking to rectify the issue. Their transparency helped maintain customer loyalty despite the crisis.

Step 4: Offer Solutions

Negative feedback or online crises are easier to navigate when you offer clear solutions. Whether it's providing compensation, fixing the issue, or explaining the corrective measures you're taking, always aim to turn a negative experience into a positive resolution.

Turning Criticism into Community Building

Negative feedback, when handled correctly, can be transformed into an opportunity to strengthen your community. By responding with kindness, professionalism, and a solutions-oriented approach, you show your audience that you value their input and are committed to growth.

- **Example:** A fitness influencer faced backlash for promoting a product that some followers found unethical. Instead of becoming defensive, they invited followers to have an open dialogue about the issue in their comments. They also organized a live Q&A session to discuss the situation and promised to be more mindful in future partnerships. The influencer's transparency and willingness to listen deepened their relationship with their audience.

Strategies to Manage Negative Feedback

1. **Respond Promptly:** Timely responses show that you're paying attention and that you value feedback. Acknowledge the issue as soon as possible, even if you don't have a full resolution yet.

2. **Stay Calm and Composed:** Don't let emotions drive your response. Stay

professional, polite, and solution-oriented.

3. **Take the Conversation Offline:** If a situation escalates or requires more detailed conversation, invite the person to discuss the matter privately through direct messages, emails, or phone calls. This helps resolve the issue in a less public setting.

4. **Learn and Improve:** Negative feedback can reveal areas where you can improve. Take the opportunity to review internal processes, products, or services and make changes where needed.

5. **Monitor Your Brand Reputation:** Use tools like Google Alerts, Social Mention, or Hootsuite to keep track of mentions of your brand. Being aware of what's being said helps you stay ahead of potential issues.

- Action Items: Handling Negative Feedback and Online Crises

- **Develop a Crisis Plan:** Create a social media crisis management plan outlining steps to take in the event of a negative situation. Include guidelines for who responds, how quickly, and what tone to use.

1. **Identify Common Types of Negative Feedback:** Make a list of the most common types of feedback you receive—whether it's about products, services, or customer support. Have prepared responses for each that reflect empathy and professionalism.

2. **Monitor Your Online Presence:** Use monitoring tools to track mentions of your brand and industry keywords. Regularly review social media comments, reviews, and messages to catch potential issues early.

3. **Practice Composure:** When responding to criticism, practice taking a deep breath and crafting thoughtful, calm responses. Avoid getting defensive or emotional—focus on solutions and customer care.

4. **Turn Criticism into Conversations:** Approach negative feedback as an opportunity to engage in meaningful dialogue with your audience. Use these moments to show transparency and your commitment to learning from mistakes.

5. **Learn from Past Mistakes:** Reflect on previous instances of negative feedback or crises. What worked well in your response? What could you improve? Continuously refine your approach to become more resilient and responsive.

Handling negative feedback and online crises is an inevitable part of growing your presence online. But with the right approach, these challenges can be transformed into opportunities to deepen trust, strengthen your community, and refine your business. Stay resilient, stay kind, and always keep the bigger picture in mind—every experience is a chance to learn, grow, and move closer to your goals.

Chapter 12: The Future of Social Media for Small Businesses

"With the growing reliance on social media, we no longer search for news or the products and services we wish to purchase. Instead, they are pushed to us by friends, colleagues, and acquaintances."

-Erick Qualman

The world of social media is constantly evolving, offering small businesses unprecedented opportunities to grow, connect, and thrive. What once started as a way for friends and family to stay in touch has now transformed into a powerful tool for businesses of all sizes to build brands, engage with customers, and drive revenue. And while the landscape may be ever-changing, one thing remains constant: the potential for small businesses to succeed on social media has never been greater.

In this chapter, we will explore the future of social media for small businesses, highlighting emerging trends, new tools, and strategies that will help you stay ahead of the curve. As technology advances and customer expectations shift, small businesses that remain adaptable, innovative, and intentional in their social media approach will lead the way. Whether you're just starting out or looking to take your brand to the next level, the future of social media offers endless possibilities.

The Rise of Short-Form Video

In recent years, short-form video content has taken the social media world by storm. Platforms like TikTok, Instagram Reels, and YouTube Shorts have revolutionized how people consume content, offering bite-sized, entertaining, and informative videos that capture attention quickly. For small businesses, this trend presents a golden opportunity to showcase products, services, and brand stories in creative ways that resonate with audiences.

The future of social media will see an even greater emphasis on short-form video, and businesses that master this format will thrive. The key is to focus on authenticity and relatability. People want to see real stories, real people, and behind-the-scenes glimpses of your business. You don't need a massive budget or professional equipment—what matters most is the connection you create with your audience.

Example: A Small Bakery's Viral Success

A small bakery in New York City started posting 15-second videos of their daily pastry creations on TikTok. These videos were simple, featuring time-lapsed footage of croissants being folded or cookies being freshly baked. The authenticity of the content quickly gained attention, and within months, the bakery's follower count exploded, leading to increased foot traffic and online orders.

What This Means for You: Small businesses have the power to go viral by showcasing what makes them unique. Short-form video allows you to tell your brand's story in a digestible, captivating way, no matter your industry.

Social Commerce: A New Era of Online Shopping

Social commerce, the integration of shopping experiences directly into social media platforms, is transforming the way consumers discover and purchase products. As platforms like Instagram, Facebook, Pinterest, and TikTok continue to develop seamless shopping experiences, the future of e-commerce will be deeply intertwined with social media.

For small businesses, this means an opportunity to turn engagement into revenue in real time. Instead of directing customers away from social media to make a purchase, social commerce allows your audience to browse, shop, and buy without leaving the platform. This is a game-changer for small businesses that want to leverage their social media presence to drive sales.

Example: A Boutique Clothing Brand's Instagram Shop

A boutique clothing brand leveraged Instagram's shopping feature to tag their products directly in posts, stories, and Reels. Followers could click on an item they liked, view details, and purchase without leaving the app. This reduced friction in the buying process and increased conversion rates. By combining visually appealing content with the convenience of social commerce, the boutique saw a significant rise in sales, particularly among mobile users.

What This Means for You: Small businesses should embrace social commerce to simplify the buying process and maximize sales potential. Whether you sell handmade jewelry, digital products, or services, social media platforms are becoming one-stop shops for engagement and transactions.

AI and Personalization: Crafting Tailored Experiences

Artificial Intelligence (AI) is already making waves in social media, and its influence will only grow in the future. AI is helping businesses analyze data, understand customer behavior, and create personalized experiences. For small businesses, this means greater efficiency and the ability to offer highly relevant content to each individual follower or customer.

AI-driven personalization tools can suggest the best times to post, create automated replies for customer inquiries, and even analyze which types of content are performing best. With AI, small businesses can deliver the right message to the right audience at the right time, enhancing engagement and building stronger customer relationships.

Example: A Coffee Shop's AI-Enhanced Social Media Strategy

A local coffee shop used AI to analyze customer engagement data from their Instagram account. The AI tool helped them identify the best times to post and suggested which types of content (behind-the-scenes videos, customer testimonials, etc.) generated the most engagement. Over time, the coffee shop refined their social media strategy, leading to increased visibility and customer loyalty.

What This Means for You: AI tools can help small businesses maximize their social media impact by offering personalized content and automating time-consuming tasks. By embracing AI, you can save time and deliver more targeted, engaging experiences to your followers.

Building Communities Through Niche Platforms

While major platforms like Facebook, Instagram, and TikTok dominate the social media space, niche platforms are rising in popularity. Platforms like Discord, Reddit, and Clubhouse offer unique ways to build tight-knit communities around specific interests. For small businesses, the future of social media lies not just in reaching the largest audience but in building meaningful relationships within niche communities.

By joining or creating groups on niche platforms, small businesses can engage in deeper, more personalized conversations with their audience. These platforms often allow for more intimate interactions, fostering a sense of belonging and loyalty.

Example: A Fitness Trainer on Discord

A fitness trainer launched a private Discord server for their clients and followers. In this community, they shared workout tips, nutrition advice, and hosted live Q&A sessions. The trainer's clients felt like they were part of a close-knit group, and the sense of community kept engagement high. This helped the trainer not only retain existing clients but also attract new ones through word-of-mouth.

What This Means for You: Small businesses should explore niche platforms to foster deeper connections with their audience. Whether it's creating a private group or hosting exclusive content, niche platforms allow you to build trust and loyalty with your most dedicated followers.

The Importance of Authenticity and Purpose

As the future of social media unfolds, one thing remains clear: authenticity will continue to be the cornerstone of successful social media strategies. Today's consumers value transparency, ethics, and purpose-driven brands. Small businesses that stay true to their values and openly share their journey will thrive in the evolving social media landscape.

People want to connect with brands that align with their values. Whether it's sharing your brand's mission, sustainability efforts, or personal stories, being authentic will help you stand out in a crowded digital world.

Example: A Sustainable Beauty Brand's Transparent Journey

A small, sustainable beauty brand shared their journey of sourcing eco-friendly materials, using recyclable packaging, and giving back to the environment. Through Instagram stories, blog posts, and behind-the-scenes videos, they brought customers along for the ride. This transparency built a strong emotional connection with their audience, and the brand saw increased engagement and customer loyalty.

What This Means for You: As social media becomes more saturated, staying true to your values and sharing your authentic story will be key to standing out. Don't be afraid to showcase your business's purpose and mission—your audience will appreciate your honesty.

Action Items: Preparing for the Future of Social Media

1. **Create Short-Form Videos:** Start experimenting with TikTok, Instagram Reels, or YouTube Shorts to showcase your products or services in a fun, authentic way. Aim to post one video per week and track engagement to see what resonates with your audience.

2. **Set Up Social Commerce Features:** If applicable, activate the shopping features on platforms like Instagram, Facebook, or Pinterest. Ensure your product catalog is up to date and easy to navigate. Test shoppable posts and track the results.

3. **Incorporate AI Tools:** Explore AI-driven tools like Later, Hootsuite, or Buffer to analyze your social media data and automate routine tasks. Experiment with AI chatbots to handle customer inquiries efficiently.

4. **Join a Niche Platform:** Consider joining or creating a community on a niche platform like Discord, Reddit, or Clubhouse. Engage with like-minded individuals and offer exclusive content to deepen relationships.

5. **Share Your Authentic Story:** Post about your brand's mission, values, and journey. Be transparent about your business's challenges and triumphs. Authenticity builds trust and long-term customer loyalty.

The future of social media for small businesses is filled with exciting opportunities. By embracing short-form video, social commerce, AI, niche platforms, and authenticity, you can stay ahead of the curve and create meaningful connections with your audience. The key is to remain adaptable, curious, and committed to growth—just as the social media landscape evolves, so too can your business. The possibilities are endless, and with the right strategies, your business can engage, thrive, and succeed in the future of social media.

Conclusion: Engage, Thrive, and Lead the Way Forward

"The more passionate and narrative I get the more followers and friends I make online."

-Tasha Turner

As we reach the conclusion of *Engage and Thrive: A Guide to Building a Strong Online Community of Raving Fans*, it's important to take a moment to reflect on how far you've come. Social media is not just a tool—it's a landscape of endless possibilities for building meaningful connections, growing your business, and making a positive impact on the world. The strategies, insights, and tips you've learned throughout this book are designed to empower you to build a thriving online community that not only supports your business but also ignites your passion and purpose.

The Power of Connection

At the heart of every successful social media strategy is the power of connection. Social media allows you to reach beyond the limitations of geography and time, giving you access to a global audience, niche markets, and loyal customers. But more than that, it allows you to foster relationships with real people who care about what you do and who are invested in your journey.

These connections aren't just about likes, shares, or comments—they are about building a community of people who believe in your mission, resonate with your message, and feel like they are a part of something bigger. When you approach social media with the mindset of connection over promotion, you unlock the true potential of these platforms. Your followers become more than just numbers on a screen—they become raving fans, ambassadors of your brand, and even partners in your growth.

Remember: It's not just about the content you create, but the relationships you nurture. Every comment, every message, and every interaction is an opportunity to deepen a connection with someone who can be a part of your long-term success.

Embrace Authenticity and Purpose

One of the recurring themes in this book is the importance of being authentic. In a world saturated with content, the businesses and brands that stand out are the ones that dare to be real, vulnerable, and transparent. Authenticity is your superpower—it's what will set you apart from the competition and resonate deeply with your audience.

In the future of social media, where people are becoming increasingly discerning, authenticity and purpose-driven content will matter more than ever. People want to support brands that align with their values and contribute to something positive in the world. Whether you're selling a product, offering a service, or building a personal brand, your audience needs to know the "why" behind your business.

What impact are you trying to make? What values do you stand by? What stories define your brand's journey?

When you can communicate your purpose with clarity and conviction, you inspire loyalty, trust, and advocacy. People want to be part of a movement, and by aligning your brand with a purpose that matters to both you and your audience, you create a sense of community that transcends mere transactions.

Actionable Thought: Take some time to reflect on your brand's purpose. Write it down, revisit it often, and let it guide your social media content. Your purpose is the foundation on which your thriving community will be built.

Adapt, Innovate, and Stay Resilient

Social media is constantly evolving. New platforms emerge, algorithms change, trends shift—but what remains constant is the need to adapt and stay resilient. The businesses that thrive in this dynamic environment are the ones that embrace change, try new things, and aren't afraid to fail forward.

You may encounter challenges along the way—whether it's a dip in engagement, a negative comment, or a new platform that feels overwhelming to navigate. But every challenge is also an opportunity for growth. When things don't go according to plan, see it as a chance to learn, tweak your strategy, and come back stronger. Keep experimenting, stay curious, and trust that your persistence will pay off in the long run.

Remember: Innovation happens when you step outside of your comfort zone and dare to try something new. Whether it's adopting a new content strategy, diving into short-form video, or launching a user-generated content campaign, be willing to evolve alongside the platforms and your audience.

Actionable Thought: Ask yourself, "Where can I innovate?" Identify one area in your social media strategy where you can try something new. Challenge yourself to experiment with a fresh approach and embrace the lessons that come with it.

Celebrate Your Wins, Big and Small

Building a successful social media presence takes time, effort, and consistency. Along the way, it's easy to get caught up in chasing big numbers or comparing your progress to others. But success isn't just about hitting a certain number of followers or going viral—it's about the small, meaningful wins that you achieve along the way.

Did you receive a heartfelt message from a follower who was inspired by your post? Did your community engage in a thoughtful conversation around one of your values? Did a piece of content resonate with a new audience?

These are all moments of success that deserve to be celebrated. Every step forward, no matter how small, is a victory. When you shift your focus to celebrating these wins, you build positive momentum that fuels your journey. Gratitude for the present moment will propel you forward as you continue to grow and evolve.

Remember: Success isn't a destination—it's a journey. Appreciate the progress you're making today, and trust that it will lead you to even greater achievements tomorrow.

Actionable Thought: Create a "win log" where you document your successes, no matter how small. Reflect on these wins regularly to stay motivated and remind yourself of how far you've come.

Your Social Media Journey is Just Beginning

The strategies you've learned in this book are just the beginning of your social media journey. The real magic happens when you put them into action, stay consistent, and continue learning along the way. Building a thriving online community doesn't happen overnight—but with patience, persistence, and passion, the results will come.

Social media is an incredible tool for growth, not just for your business but for your personal development as well. Every post, every interaction, and every piece of content is an opportunity for you to learn more about yourself, your audience, and your mission. By showing up with intention and authenticity, you're not just building a business—you're building a legacy.

So, as you move forward, remember to trust the process. Stay connected to your purpose. Keep adapting, innovating, and learning. Celebrate your wins, and don't be afraid to take risks. You are capable of creating a community of raving fans who believe in what you do—and with the strategies in this book, you have everything you need to make that vision a reality.

Final Action Steps: Thriving Beyond the Book

To help you get started on this next chapter of your journey, here are a few final action steps:

1. **Define Your Purpose:** Take time to clarify the core purpose of your business and how it aligns with the values of your audience. Let this purpose guide your

social media content and interactions moving forward.

2. **Experiment with New Platforms:** Consider experimenting with new platforms or formats to expand your reach. Whether it's trying TikTok, launching a podcast, or diving into Instagram Reels, don't be afraid to explore new territories.

3. **Commit to Consistency:** Building a thriving community requires showing up consistently. Create a social media schedule that works for you, and commit to regular posting, engagement, and community building.

4. **Celebrate Progress:** Keep track of your wins, big and small. Whether it's a new follower, a meaningful comment, or a successful post, celebrate your progress and use it as fuel for the journey ahead.

5. **Engage with Your Community:** Social media isn't just about broadcasting—it's about engaging. Dedicate time to listen to your audience, respond to comments, and participate in conversations that matter to your community.

Your journey to engaging and thriving on social media is filled with endless possibilities. The future belongs to those who dare to lead with authenticity, innovate with courage, and nurture connections with intention. Now is your time to not only succeed but to thrive—and to build a community that will stand with you every step of the way.

Here's to your social media success and the incredible journey ahead! Keep engaging, keep thriving, and let your brand shine.

PLEASE DO ME A HUGE FAVOR

Please do me a huge favor, if you have been inspired by my books and want to help others to reach their goals and improve their lives too, here are some action steps you can take immediately to make a positive difference:

Write a review on Amazon for this book. Reviews are critical for authors, helping us sell more books and deliver more value to our readers. It also helps people looking for my books, find them more easily. People are more apt to buy a book like this if there are positive reviews telling them how the book has helped its readers personally.

Gift my books. Gift my books to friends, family, colleagues and even strangers so that they can also learn how create social media that engages their followers and helps their businesses thrive.

Share your thoughts. Please share your thoughts about this book on X, Facebook, Instagram, LinkedIn, or any other of your favorite social media platforms or write a book review and share it. It helps other people find *Engage and Thrive* and my other books as well.

Amazon Author Page: https://www.amazon.com/stores/Veronica-Goldspiel/author/B0D466HRG9

Thank you! I can't wait to hear how *Engage and Thrive* has helped you to achieve your business goals. Please write to me and let me know all about your successes! I look forward to hearing from you. You can contact me at Veronica@GoldspielCreativeEnterprises.com.

REMINDER

FREE GIFTS JUST FOR YOU!

I also want to take this time to remind you about the FREE GIFTS I've created just for readers of this book. As a thank you for your support, I invite you to download some exciting FREE gifts that I've created to enhance your journey! Simply visit the link below to access exclusive resources designed just for you!

Your complimentary gifts include:

Engage and Thrive Cheat Sheet – This is your quick-reference guide to social media success! This valuable resource keeps essential strategies top of mind—from defining goals and knowing your audience to creating engaging content and managing feedback. Use it to stay focused on building a loyal, active community that drives your brand forward!

Handling Negative Feedback Cheat Sheet – This your essential resource for staying poised and professional in the face of criticism! This quick guide serves as a valuable reminder of key steps to take when managing feedback—from acknowledging concerns to turning insights into improvement. Keep it handy to protect your brand's reputation while building stronger relationships through thoughtful responses!

Social Proof Cheat Sheet for Small Businesses – This is your must-have guide to boosting credibility and trust with potential customers! This valuable resource covers key ways to gather and showcase authentic feedback, testimonials, and influencer endorsements that make your brand stand out. Keep it on hand to easily remind yourself of proven strategies that build customer confidence and drive sales!

30-Day Social Media Content Calendar Cheat Sheet – This is your ultimate roadmap to creating meaningful, high-engagement content every day! This valuable resource will keep you inspired with fresh ideas that foster connection, showcase your brand, and build an active, thriving community. It's the perfect guide to remind you of key strategies and take your social presence to the next level!

GET YOUR FREE GIFTS NOW BY GOING TO: https://goldspielcreativeenterprises.com/free-gifts-engage-and-thrive/

CONNECT WITH ME ON FACEBOOK!

Join my *Small Business Wealth Marketing* private Facebook community here: https://www.facebook.com/groups/smallbusinesswealthmarketing

I also invite you to engage with me on my Official Veronica Goldspiel Author Facebook Page here: https://www.facebook.com/veronicagoldspielauthor/

ABOUT THE AUTHOR

Photo Credit: Dr. Alan Goldspiel

eronica Goldspiel, a #1 best-selling author and veteran freelancer with over two decades of experience, has worked with top motivational and self-improvement speakers worldwide, including luminaries like Tony Robbins and T. Harv Eker.

Veronica's expertise spans various sectors, from healthcare to entertainment, and offers a holistic approach to business and personal growth. Her extensive skills in social media management, content creation, and book publishing as well as health and wellness continue to empower clients globally.

As an author, Veronica penned works such as her #1 Best Sellers *Freelance Success Secrets: 21 Essential Habits That Will Transform Your Freelance Business From Surviving to Thriving*, *Dream Catchers: Mastering the Art of Realizing Your Dreams* and *From Likes to Profits: A Guide to Choosing the Most Profitable Social Media Platforms for Your Brand*. She is also the author of *Finance for Freelancers: Maximize Income, Manage Cash Flow, Minimize Stress*, *Reflections for Dream Catchers: The Inspirational Book of*

Wisdom for Your Journey to Success, and *Making Your Business a Social Media Superstar: A Step-by-Step Guide to Creating, Maintaining, and Promoting Your Online Presence.* You can connect with Veronica at: www.goldspielcreativeenterprises.com

Her commitment to sharing knowledge extends beyond books, as she regularly contributes to platforms like www.thefreelancerslife.com.

Driven by a passion to empower others, Veronica focuses on producing books across her many areas of expertise to aid individuals in overcoming their challenges and to more easily achieve their aspirations. When she's not immersed in writing, Veronica can be found honing her barista skills with her espresso machine, engrossed in a good read, or enjoying beach outings with her husband, Alan.

You can connect with Veronica at: www.goldspielcreativeenterprises.com.

Her Amazon Author Page is here: https://www.amazon.com/stores/Veronica-Goldspiel/author/B0D466HRG9

Veronica Goldspiel Official Facebook Page: https://www.facebook.com/veronicagoldspielauthor

OTHER BOOKS BY AUTHOR

Finance for Freelancers: Maximize Income, Manage Cash Flow, Minimize Stress (The Freelancer's Life Series)

Freelance Success Secrets: 21 Essential Habits That Will Transform Your Freelance Business From Surviving to Thriving (The Freelancer's Life Series)

Reflections for Dream Catchers: The Inspirational Book of Wisdom for Your Journey to Success (Personal Growth and Motivation Series)

Dream Catchers: Mastering the Art of Realizing Your Dreams (Personal Growth and Motivation Series)

From Likes to Profits: A Guide to Choosing the Most Profitable Social Media Platforms for Your Brand (Small Business Wealth Marketing Series)

Making Your Business a Social Media Superstar: The Step-by-Step Guide to Creating, Maintaining, and Promoting Your Online Presence (as Veronica Buhl)

The Massage Disadvantage: What Doctors Know About Making Money That Massage Therapists Don't! (Co-Author as Veronica Buhl)

www.ingramcontent.com/pod-product-compliance
Lightning Source LLC
LaVergne TN
LVHW051847080426
835512LV00018B/3116